HERE COMES
THE ASSEMBLY MAN
A Year in the Life of a Primary School

Fred Sedgwick

 The Falmer Press

(A member of the Taylor & Francis Group)
London ● New York ● Philadelphia

UK   The Falmer Press, Falmer House, Barcombe, Lewes, East Sussex
BN8 5DL

USA   The Falmer Press, Taylor & Francis Inc., 1900 Frost Road
Suite 101, Bristol, PA 19007

First published 1989

British Library Cataloguing in Publication Data

Sedgwick, Fred
    Here comes the assembly man: a year in the life of a primary
    school. − (School development and the management of change
    series; 2)
    1. Great Britain. Primary Schools. Management
    I. Title   II. Series
    372.12'00941

ISBN 1−85000−680−6
ISBN 1−85000−681−4 pbk

Typeset in 12/13 Garamond by
The FD Group Ltd, Fleet, Hampshire

Printed in Great Britain by Taylor and Francis (Printers) Ltd,
Basingstoke

Contents

Acknowledgments

I would like to thank the staff at Cowper County Primary School for their help; also Geoff Southworth, whose help and encouragment kept me going.

Five paragraphs of this book have appeared, in different forms, in *The Times Educational Supplement* and in *Art and Craft*.

The two songs quoted are from *Wake Up Stir About* (Unwin Hyman). 'Child asks . . ' was first published in the *School's Poetry Review*. 'The Fight' and 'At the School Disco' appeared in *This Way That Way* (Mary Glasgow Publications).

I am grateful to John Cotton for permission to print his riddle, and to Joy Thorn for writing part of Chapter 4.

Headmasters are always very proud of their skools and think they are the best in the world in britain in space or at any rate better than the nearest one in the districk.

(Geoffrey Willans and Ronald Searle
Down with skool, Fontana)

The children their unsmiling kingdoms keep,
And I walk with them, and I am afraid.

(Charles Causley, *Collected Poems*, Macmillan)

In Memory of
Justin Andrews (1981-1988)

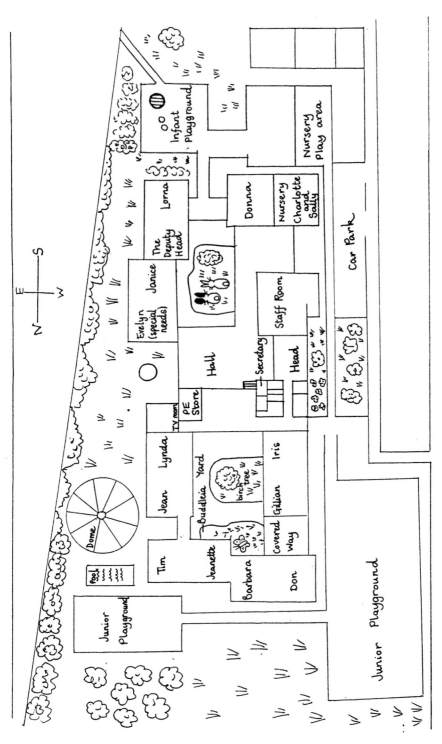

Map 1: Cowper School (January–July)

(Drawn by Lorraine Rainbow)

Introduction

Cowper (pronounced 'Cooper') County Primary School was planned in the mid-1960s in the days of the Beatles and the Plowden Report. This was before anyone, even an education officer, knew there was going to be an oil crisis, a recession, or a sudden decline in the birthrate. So this single-storey school has much glass in its construction, a feeling of sufficient light and air; and consequent heating problems. It has corridors and classrooms of generous size, two halls, one of them a grey dome, common in the area, separated from the main building; two 'general purpose' areas and an audiovisual room that doubles as an instrumental teaching area. Cowper also has extensive grounds, including shrubs (lilac, laburnum, rose, forsythia) and trees — although many of these are sycamore, irritatingly resistant (it turned out in October 1987) to hurricane, and maddeningly efficient breeders. The main physical feature as you cross the inadequate car park is an ash-coloured wooden fascia that surrounds much of the glass. As functional 1960s buildings go, Cowper is a more than decent example (see Map 1).

The school was opened on St George's Day, 1968. This is also Shakespeare's birthday as well as the anniversary of his death, but the temptation to give the school a patriotic or Shakespearean name was resisted. The roads around here are all named after other poets, and all the city's schools are named after their roads. An earlier head introduced the hare as the school's badge (the poet, William Cowper, 1731-1799, kept hares, and wrote one of his most famous poems about the death of one) and a flag with a stylized hare motif flies over the school on high days, such as Cowper's birthday (15 November), his anniversary (25 April), the beginnings and ends of terms, and the evenings of plays and concerts. The hare is prominent on the children's scarlet jumpers, that have largely taken the place of a school uniform. It also decorates the headed notepaper.

If you are used to Victorian school buildings, all too often entirely innocent of grass, or with little light, you feel grateful for schools like Cowper. The school's structural problems are relatively minor, and do not seriously affect the children. There is a lack of storage space, admittedly, and costly heating that, in the cold moments of the more severe months of the English winter, leaves classrooms with temperatures that few office workers would tolerate. There is also a ludicrous shortage of ladies' lavatories. But mostly, Cowper's anxieties come from a different quarter: vandalism and break-ins are endemic to the area, and over the past four years there have been many occasions when the main business of the morning for head and secretary has been talking to the police and the local press, and filling in insurance claims, after the loss of a video, some panelling to the covered swimming pool, calculators or, saddest of all, the exotic-looking fish in the tank that used to stand in the entrance hall. If the school feels open to parents, it also feels open to casual crooks, and ex-pupils beginning a training in their craft.

The 390 children are arranged like this: in a nursery with fifty half-time places; six infant classes; three lower junior ones; and three upper junior ones. It is clear from this balance that the decline of the previous years has finished, and that there is, in fact, a slight growth at the younger end of the school. There are no places available in reception classes for any children living outside the catchment area, even if they have attended the nursery, and even if their parents have put forward a strong case to the authority.

In the social sense of the word, there have been dramatic changes in the class of the children attending Cowper over the past ten years. When my predecessor took up the headship in 1978, the main catchment area was a group of roads with royal names (Princess, Windsor, Hanover, Balmoral) and fairly high aspirations. Almost no children come from there now: these villas are out of reach of most young families. Cowper's clients today come mostly from houses built in the 1980s — and very different they are too. Thirty yards away from my office, where my predecessor could stand and look out over fields bright with bluetits, goldcrests and chaffinches, there is a row of terraced dwellings. If you live in one and your cat dies, you do not swing it about. In the sort of space that accommodates a garden for one of the big houses on nearby Spenser Road, the council has fitted in some thirty 'living units' — and for once the ugly officialese is entirely appropriate.

The usual litany of problems has come with these houses: unemployment, single parenthood, domestic violence, adolescent boredom. On bright evenings from early April to late September, local young men hang around, or bang a football against the brick walls in Cowper Drive. Some of them are married, and will soon be Cowper parents; others left the school only two or three years ago, and they clamber on to the fence and sit there, shouting and smoking. Girls lean around the place, too, waiting for something to happen.

Cowper Drive is without any doubt the road where my reputation is lowest. This may be because of the heavy line I took when I first came here about children playing in the school grounds after school hours. Or it may be that the road is a difficult road in a general way, and that the perpetrators of the break-ins come from the close vicinity of the school — or that those closest see most clearly the weaknesses in a headteacher's relations with the children. Anyway, several of these families send their children to nearby Edinburgh Road School, following noisy disagreements with me.

Immediately opposite my office is Craig's house. He always made me think of a troublesome squaddie, with his close-cropped hair and his habit of saying 'Right Sir' whenever I asked him to stop beating Simon Jewson up, or swearing at Mrs Caldicott, one of the dinner ladies. When he left, it was a relief. Tim Kite once wrote a cod report on him that said simply, 'I can't wait to get rid of the little sod.' He once spent a happy minute chucking stones at a crossing patrol from the embankment above Tennyson Road. His unemployed older brother plays pop records very loudly from his bedroom on warm days, the window wide open. The Smiddies, next door, left when I closed the tuck shop. Mr. Carstairs has done time for beating his women up. On the other hand, there are fiercely respectable families in the road as well, like the Eagletons, whose daughter Sarah is brilliant on the cello, and whose son is a fine footballer, and Chris Gaynor, cheerfully on her own, whose family adore her.

There are other roads like this, then quieter ones, also composed of council houses, then a large private estate of three and four bedroomed properties that Cowper shares with Edinburgh Road School: all open-plan, shaved front lawns and carriage lamps. On this estate are the only churches and pubs in the neighbourhood: you can sense a certain heartlessness that stems from a lack of these facilities around Cowper School. Some of the children living here who should go to Edinburgh Road come to Cowper.

This study of one year in the life of Cowper School will concentrate on the children and their learning: the curriculum in the widest sense of the word — all the experiences the children have in the place between coming to school fifteen minutes before official opening time and going home sometime between 3.30 and 4.00. Most of the account will concentrate on teachers relating to children in classrooms, on playgrounds, on field trips, at concerts, etc. I am going to avoid teachers' personalities for three reasons: first, I do not want to embarrass myself or my colleagues; second, I want to get essentially educational moments into focus, and have noticed how too strong a light on teachers' personalities prevents this; and third, the notion of teachers' biographies is being looked at by many other writers. Some of this work is academic in character (at the Cambridge Institute of Education, for example); some of it has been in fiction, such as J.L. Carr's *The Harpole Report* and G.W. Target's *The Teachers*.

Sometimes fictional work of this kind has been so witty as to offer alarming insights into the nature of the British primary school (Carr); sometimes the results have been melodramatic, like a foreshortened soap opera, as in Target. Either way, I did not want to tread the same ground — or, come to that, ground examined so illuminatingly by books like Edward Blishen's sequence of memoirs about teaching, or Gwen Dunn's *Simon's Last Year*, about a village school in the 1950s, not a million miles from Cowper; or Joan Goldman's *Brave New School*. I would be proud if it was thought that my story complements these books with a perspective which is neither fictional nor academic, but which owes much to those approaches in an attempt 'to get under the skin' of one large urban primary.

When I do look at the teachers, it will be in terms of their relationships with the children, rather than as they are in the staffroom, in their usually amiable, occasionally very close, and only rarely fraught colleague relationships. The following brief sketch of the staffroom is intended to give some backdrop to the main events going on centre stage, where the children and the teachers 'interact' (as most of us have learned to say nowadays).

Cowper is a comfortable school. Some staff have stayed over ten years, and it is mainly these who run the social life of the place. The room itself has the air of a club at times, with certain high points of the year celebrated with a combination of vitality and efficiency. Staff Christmas lunch, for example, is gastronomically and conversationally a vivid event, as are meals at the ends of other terms. Many of the staff are involved in a local amateur dramatic society that mounts its plays in the school hall, and this group provides a social centre for the staff's activities.

As well as the children and the staff, I will describe the school's constantly changing encounter with its community through the PTA; through more formal parent-teacher contacts; and through any other events that might involve the school — visits to the town, and visits from agencies such as the police. And, of course, I am concerned with the local education authority (LEA): a decent one to work for. The advisers have always been humane and humorous, and the officers immaculate in their deployment of the increasingly meagre resources allotted them by central government. The official curriculum papers were prepared by teachers alongside advisers, and reflect both classroom reality and the power, in the early 1980s, of the objectives movement in curriculum design. There have been lively initiatives about multicultural education and gender equality that set it apart from other LEAs. Democratization of governing bodies scarcely needed the government initiatives of the late 1980s.

The year I am going to describe — 1988 — exists, like any other, against the background of other years, in particular the one before, which had been eventful. In May, Cowper had been inspected by local advisers for a fortnight, and the recommendations of this review were about to be put into practice. This had been traumatic for some of the staff (including me) who were not used to being watched while they were teaching. The personal style of one of the advisers upset a few of us. Here is a description of him at work from an article I published (with his permission) in the *Cambridge Journal of Education:*

> . . . the LEA descended on the school in the person of an adviser . . . [who] shook things up with his jovial but nonetheless confrontational style . . .:

> *Adviser* That Jesus story in assembly — do you tell Mohammed stories as well?
> *Head* Oh yes, I have a book of heroes of the world's religions —
> *Adviser* Tokenism!

. . . This man . . . specialised in heads-I-win-tails-you-lose questions, and dominated the school, at least on the first morning of the review, like a tall centre-half on a windy Saturday afternoon.

More important than this adviser was the long-term effect of the inspection, spreading backwards and forwards. A note I sent round six weeks before the review began gives a flavour of the preparation:

We will put in the staffroom a box which by the first day of next term will contain broad forecasts for every class . . . Each of us should make sure we read everybody else's forecasts to ensure continuity and knowledge about the school. This becomes school policy from the beginning of next term. Curriculum papers . . . should be with me, please, by April 3 so that Sue can type them up by April 8 when I have to hand them over to M [the adviser referred to earlier] . . . Please ensure that you read all these documents. The review team will be checking that the spirit (at least) and (occasionally) the content of these papers is reflected in the classrooms. They may become discussion papers for development . . . PLEASE KEEP THIS FILE INTACT . . .

Anyone who would like a conversation about his/her work/career . . . should ask the review team leader [M] . . .

The team will need a timetable from each of you. Where you run an integrated day, please write 'integrated' in the relevant place. Please make sure the hall, dome and tv places are marked and largely adhered to . . .

The following offer is still open — anyone who wants to try to predict advisers' comments . . . should see me to discuss the matter. This should be a good opportunity to put a few small things right before they come . . .

If the school had existed as an isolated entity, clearly that could not happen after 1988. For one reason, the review had brought to bear upon the staff what the LEA wanted (though the LEA's power was perceptibly diminishing). Second, the school-centred INSET arrangements (which were coming into force at this time) insisted on teachers talking with others in local schools about the needs of the group. This led to meeting after meeting, as teachers accepted, with varying degrees of willingness, the responsibility of designing their own in-service work. Third, of course, national politics affected education so that it was no longer possible to say that the two things could be separated. National Curriculum, testing, the almost certainly anti-democratic effects of centralization: all this became a matter for consideration at staff meetings, and some teachers connected the effect of government policies with the also current cowing of the BBC, the starving of the arts, and the disempowerment of the National Health Service. Some headteachers also felt that the deflection of their attentions away from children towards the financial management of their schools was part of the same movement, and were puzzled by the fact that this was Labour Party as well as Government policy.

National politics tended to unite post-Plowden teachers, who felt that open enrolment and the centralized, monitored curriculum would work against schools like Cowper, where county test scores were certainly no better than average, and where teaching of the arts (an area largely sidelined in official documents) was lively, imaginative and rated important. Another decision made at Whitehall was seen as relevant: almost all teachers believed they had been robbed of their status along with their negotiating rights, which had disappeared in the backwash of the pay dispute.

Local events in 1987 had included the loss of two lively members of staff, and their replacement with two equally lively probationers (Jeanette and Donna); the transfer of another teacher (Charlotte) from a reception class to the nursery; a few dismally attended dances, that were like parties held in a barn, only worse, because you had to pay for your drinks; and the theft of £400 from the secretary's desk on election day, probably by an itinerant voter. There was a cynical consensus among some of the staff as to how this extremely private enterprise leaning individual had voted. 'What's the difference', said someone, 'whether you pinch cash from the office, or parts of the capitation? . . .'

This account of 1988 is made up of fieldnotes and comments on them; contributions from children, teachers, parents and governors; correspondence, poems, drawings, minutes and reports. It is an attempt to portray life in a large school from the head's point of view. I told the staff at the beginning of the year that I was writing this book, and that their names would be changed; and that they would be able to see the rough drafts whenever they wanted. Several have, therefore, read all or part of the material, and some of their suggested alterations are now part of the story.

Some of what happened was too dramatic for art — who would have believed in the corkscrew incident (Chapter 1) had it appeared in a novel? But everybody knows from experience how strange truth is. Most know how untidy it is, too. I hope its transformation here into something that looks like a mix of conscientious journalism, imaginative fiction, a school log and an evaluative project can be educational, as it sharpens our focus on that vital issue for our times: what happens in a school?

The *Main characters* are: Junior Teachers: Lynda (responsible for art and some music), Jean (maths), Tim (science), Barbara (implementing the National Curriculum), Don (PE and computers), Jeanette (probationer), Helena (resources).

Infant teachers: the deputy head (till July), Janice (responsible for home-school relations, and acting deputy-head after September), Gillian (music), Lorna (language), Iris (language), Donna (probationer), Anna (cover for the deputy's class after September), Miriam (the new deputy, who takes up her post after the end of the book), Charlotte (nursery, and the 'social and political'), Evelyn (special needs, and some music), Jackie (part-time).

Other staff: Sally (nursery nurse), Susie (classroom ancillary), Sue (secretary), David (caretaker), Keith (Chairman of Governors).

Some of the children: Simon (8 years), who has problems with bullying, warts, his eyesight and (his mother says) dyslexia; Danielle (9), Charlotte's daughter, who writes and dances; Pauline (10), her best friend who does too; Jeremy (7); Justin and Ben Andrews (7 and 4) and their mother; Damien (8), who gets into trouble; Mark (8), his friend (and his grandfather, Mr Leach); Sam (6), who has tooth trouble (and Carol, his mother); Shaun (6); Miranda (5); Margaret (11), who is called bad names; Stella (11), who is vegetarian; George (10); Sarah (11).

Headteachers: Reg, Jerry, Stuart, Julie, Dennis.

Almost all these names have been changed.

Chapter 1

Corkscrews (January, February)

Les choses ne sont jamais definitement en ordre (Alain Robbe-Grillet)

The drunkenness of things being various (Louis MacNeice *Collected Poems*, Faber)

In fact any skool is a bit of a shambles. AS YOU WILL SEE. (Willans and Searle)

Here comes the assembly man (child in the nursery at Cowper School)

The first half-term of the year was to end with a fight.

It's 3.20 on 19 February, the final Friday afternoon. The weather is damp and mild, germs still thriving, people say, because of the lack of a real winter. There's normally an assembly going on at this point, the aim of which is to send the children off with a sharing of work of all kinds, from throughout the school. This ritual, with its implicit humanist celebration of our own nature, often covers for religion in primary schools, but it has a good Judaeo-Christian text: 'And God saw everything that He had made, and, behold, it was very good' (Genesis 1.31). At this assembly we help children show off poems, stories, descriptions, anecdotes, paintings, models, experiments, dance, drama, and (less often) mathematics. Next, we warn the children about the traffic and other dangers; we sing a song or two, and Happy Birthday; and then, gratefully, we send them home.

But on this Friday there'd been a concert for parents in the morning, and we felt there'd been enough sitting on bottoms on cold floors for one day. And I couldn't have led assembly because the termly governors' meeting was taking place in a classroom. So, as end of day, week, half, approached, children were everywhere, in classroms, library and dining area. This last re-settles as an extension of the library outside the lunchhour.

I am with the governors talking about the Education Reform ('so-called', said Chairman Keith) Bill when Gillian, an infant teacher, breaks the seal dividing us from the real world and says, 'You'd better come outside, there's a fight going on.' And indeed, one woman is almost on top of another in the dining area, yelling something that I cannot now remember. I take her shoulders, haul her up and say stupidly, as though she'd been telling a rude joke at a church social, something about there being children around. Meanwhile another parent is taking the other woman away. She turned out to be a child-minder come to take an infant home.

I saw 11-year-old Simone's face gazing open-mouthed as she was supposed to be concentrating on *The Turbulent Term of Tyke Tyler*, and I thought, Oh well, she's seen EastEnders . . . And then I thought, did this sort of thing happen when Gwyn was in this job? Have my tie-less, informal ways led to fights on LEA premises?

I walked the first woman to her 6-year-old awestruck daughter. Sue, the secretary, took the child-minder to my office with minor wounds resulting from stabs with a corkscrew: bloody jabs in the palm of her right hand, and a seeping scratch in her left thigh. I left her with a cup of sugary tea and a cigarette that Sue gave her. It made me nostalgic for the camaraderie of nicotine, the days when a packet of twenty seemed innocent.

Back in the governors' meeting, life was less exciting. I mouthed the parent's name at one of the teachers, and she looked at me like someone asked to express extreme shock at a theatrical audition. Then I reflected on whether I'd have waded in so readily if I'd known about the corkscrew. Of course I would have. But writers about headship are adrift when they say, 'proposals . . . promised by the Education Reform Bill make the job more like a managing director, less like an educational policy director' (*The Guardian,* 31 May 1988). We are concerned all the time with human beings, and sometimes we are social workers, sometimes referees, sometimes police officers. I have been, in the last twelve years of headship (at Cowper and two other schools), not only 'educational policy director' but boiler attendant, cleaner, decorator, Master of Ceremonies, dance impresario and temporary caretaker. Now, Wendy Berliner says in *The Guardian,* we are to be financial managers, when many of us can't manage the money in our own pockets. But don't forget (I tell myself) Simone and her frightened look: the hungry sheep that look up and must be fed.

Before the first real day of term, there'd been a Baker Day. An earlier Conservative Minister of Education is linked for ever to a humane Act: this one is linked to compulsory in-service training days. A committee of six teachers from the three local primaries, Edinburgh Road, Valley and Cowper, had invited a lecturer from the local Institute of Education to talk about topic work.

Enforced education! What a peculiar notion! You can enforce schooling — in fact, enforcement is probably the first thing a Martian visitor would notice:

> Line up here in twos, girls this side, boys that . . . No Anthony, here . . . Now . . . Walk, no, WALK into the hall . . . Jeremy, I'd have hoped you'd have the manners to let Mrs Hanson go first . . . Find a space . . . I don't want to hear a sound from anyone . . . I'm going to count from one to three . . . What do you think you are doing, Michael? . . .

Well may my friend Geoff describe school assemblies, where this sort of language is more public than in classrooms, as 'a hymn, a prayer and a bollocking'. And Shaw, who had the measure of schools, commented, 'school . . . is a prison. But it is in some respects more cruel than a prison. In a prison, for instance, you are not obliged to read books written by the warders or the governor.'

But few of us pretend that education is happening in these enforced moments: it is schooling in the role that someone in power has deemed fit for us. Education, on the other hand, happens almost entirely in unstatutory moments, and by their nature these moments cannot be enforced, for children or teachers. But here we were in enforced education — only now, we were the students. The lecturer gave us a historical overview of progressivism: the Hadow Report ('a fascinating read') had been 'radical'. Other writers in the 1920s and 1930s had backed up what in the 1960s came to be seen as 'child-centred' experienced-based education.

Afterwards teachers commented on the lecture:

> If there was such a progressive consensus, why are most schools formal, even now?

> It was interesting to see things historically, which I'd not done since I left university.

> There was 'question time' listed on the blackboard, but he only left two minutes.

> I don't want [this from Jeanette, a probationer] to go back to college.

On the first real day of term I noted, I haven't done my tour of the school today . . . normally this is a priority task every morning: who's back after time off, who's got an arm in a sling, who's had a haircut, which December displays are still up . . .' I heard a probationer in another school say that her head hadn't been in her classroom since the previous term, but it was unclear whether she was boasting or complaining. Another, from a different school, said she couldn't do anything 'out of the ordinary' (it emerged she meant the sort of day when the children were not all working on the same subject at the same time) 'because my head watches everything I do.'

The tour keeps me in touch with what learning's going on. It also separates me from what some teachers call 'management' but which is really administration. A great deal of management, of one kind or another, goes on during the tour:

> Loved that assembly . . . Could you speak to Mrs Lee about Simon's sight? . . . Can I go on that course on multi-cultural, supply's automatic . . . I like that work on the stuff from the museum, could you have a word with Jeanette about it? . . . How did Jamie get that mark over his eye? . . . Could you help me write a reference for Lynda? . . . Wouldn't it be better if the speech therapist saw the children in school, they'd be more likely to keep their appointments . . .

Of course, it is not always clear who's managing who. But nothing can be usefully done by a teacher, including a headteacher, when the children are in school, unless it involves those children. Adding columns of figures, or counting the dance profits, are simply not educational tasks. Local Management of Schools may well sink this ideal — surely, though, it can't be a deliberate attempt to de-educationalize the head's job?

But I hadn't done my tour that day. Several waves had buffetted the ship before it left harbour: a teacher is away longish term, and supply cover had to be negotiated with the office and then (quite difficult these days) found; another teacher has been called for jury service from early February, and can only let me know day-by-day if she'll be in; the caretaker has applied for a job; there are several proposed absences for courses . . . So I stayed at my desk after my first assembly and planned.

One of the teachers, Don, got married in the Christmas holidays, and had been sent off on the penultimate day of term with a buffet lunch and sparkling wine (some of it rumoured to be champagne). He'd presented the nursery staff with a Jolly Pecker at this meal: a plastic male organ that clicked across the tablecloth to the shocked hilarity of everyone at that end of the table ('Oh, Don!') and cries of 'Send it up here, we haven't seen it yet' from the other. Since then he and his wife have visited Russia on their honeymoon. They went to a kindergarten ('Such dedication!' said someone). Dave told me, 'There's no art on the walls. Painting is associated with the church and all that. They have Grandfather Frost and Grandmother Frost, and there's tinsel everywhere . . .'

Now and then, in a school like ours, we drink wine, especially over the Christmas period. Maybe Glyn (my predecessor) comes and provides the excuse. Or one of us brings in a bottle to relieve a difficult Friday. Occasionally the spare tea money is blown on a box of Leibfraumilch and a pint of Valpolicella.

But in the puritan days of January there's no need for corkscrews. Teachers get back to the staffroom desperate only for their tea or coffee. They are cold, either because the heating system is inefficient, or because the head is treating the LEA's money as if it were his/her own. In some schools there are stickers on light-switches: TURN ME OFF. Staff meetings will be convened soon to denounce teachers who made phone calls before 1.00 pm, thus depriving other classes of some new equipment. The best teacher will be, in these mean days, the one whose art lessons depend on a dead wasp, a pencil, and paper scrounged from local industry's off-cut store.

The term got going. I phoned the head, Jerry, of one of our largest schools, to ask for a reference for a teacher who's done supply work with him, and who's applied for a six-hour job with us. Of course he would. Or he'd get one of his deputies to do it for him. Then, in answer to an enquiry about how things were:

> I get in every morning at 7.00. I have to! I've got five supplies in today — I ceilinged last week at seven. My first job everyday is to get bodies in front of classes, then I'll worry about the National Curriculum. I don't bother with local office, if they can't be bothered to get their switchboard open till 8.30 — I can't wait till then . . . I've got two just out of hospital, one on the verge of a nervous breakdown . . . No wonder only 30-odd applied for Eastyorkgate [another large primary in town] . . . a head of a big school has a lot on his plate these days. When we had an HMI inspection, one of them said to me that his hotel didn't do breakfast till 8.00 am. I told him, by the time you're having breakfast, mate, I've done an hour's work behind this desk!

I rang Jerry once, four years ago, at 2.30 pm, and he said, 'Can you hang on a minute, I've been trying to go to the toilet since coffee time.' Now I asked him: 'Have you applied for anything?'

'No, I'm staying here now . . . I've got my eyes set on retirement . . . I'm on the wrong side of 40, and I expect to go in nine years . . . I don't want anymore hassle than I've got here . . .'

Glyn had come to the Christmas concert, and as we talked about the National Curriculum, testing, Baker days, and so on, he'd said, 'It's all pressure on the headmaster.' Meeting other heads during Christmas shopping, I collected more examples of what one colleague called 'cataloguing the joys': 'We're opening a nursery, and I'm architect, planner and clerk of works without any extra time . . .'

This is essentially the view of developments as seen from the rank and file of the National Association of Headteachers (if the NAHT can be said to have a rank and file). It is, in part, the fruit of modern managerialism that separates heads from teachers, so that those heads don't see education being crippled by political reality, but only their own lives being messed up. But, yes the pressures on heads are greater than they used to be.

Since 1975, when I first became a head, I've been superstitious about my first teaching of the term. It's always poetry for me, much as for my friend Stuart, head at Watercombe Junior, on the other side of the estate, it's PE or games. Suppose we can't do it anymore! Even the one thing in teaching we think we're good at. As though it's a gift from some capricious fairy, rather than from God; something that only luck can keep a hold on, rather than constant refining and development. As though, as some poets believe about *their* gift, it's something that an apparently unconnected error could obliterate. As I walked across the quad, past the pollarded birch, to Jeanette's classroom, I avoided the cracks between the paving stones, and repeated a mantra from the Plowden Report underneath my breath: 'At the heart of the educational process lies the child.'

I used to take Jeanette's class, on the face of it, because she was a probationer; but more, really, because she made me welcome, and I find juniors of this age easier to teach than the equally welcoming infant probationer's reception plus children. I talked about the haiku, smacking out the syllables of each child's name with two fingers of my right hand on the palm of my left: 'Kate Brad-bu-ry? How many? Em-ma Fairs? . . .' I then suggested they write some haikus, using subjects they could see from where they were, and which, come to that, they could get up and feel. The birch, for example, just about to emerge from the worst of winter:

> There's buds on the arms
> and it smells like the colour.
> It's a petticoat.

> Fireworks upside down,
> reminds me of a nest upside down;
> half a golfball with holes in.

These were pieces by two different children. Another wrote about the rain:

> Rain lands on my window
> then bounces off through the air,
> comes back, stikes again.

And another looked at the sky:

> Clouds climb in air. Arms
> bitter, bite frosty sky. Air
> begins to climb.
> Wind blows trees side to side.
> It looks like a cradle rocking.
> Witch hands reach out.

I asked Jeanette for a note on how the session went. She wrote:

> One would expect any classroom full of children to hold a high level of

respect for their headteacher. The respect for Fred though represents something more than simple deference. The children LIKE Fred.

They are used to him coming in for an hour on Wednesdays and generally seem to enjoy his lessons. After this particular lesson I asked them what they thought . . . their reactions were mixed. Some had felt quite nervous about not being able to do what was expected of them. Others thoroughly enjoyed themselves. Those, on reflection, were the children who had written 'good' pieces.

. . . when a child offers a useful suggestion or has worked hard he offers ample praise which instills more self-esteem into the child.

I'm not sure this is much use as data. How could she say, 'the lesson was hopelessly mismatched to the class, and by his own preaching should not have been a lesson at all, but a period of time containing material growing naturally from the class's current interests'? Later in the year Jeanette was to comment on the children's writing with me, 'They write very much for you, in your style . . . it's not necessarily sincere, what they need to say to express their feelings — it's done for you and with what they think you like in mind . . . does that worry you at all?'

The reasons for the praise are twofold: first, sheer relief it's still working, and second it's commonsense — the more you reinforce the best in the children, the more likely you'll be to get even better stuff next time. So why do I hear so many discouraging remarks in classrooms: 'That's useless, Jeremy . . . What do you think you are doing? . . . Haven't you been listening at all? . . . That's not very neat, is it? . . . This book is a complete mess — what is your mother going to say on open evening? . . . Would you like to do the whole thing again?'

I did some more teaching the next day. Tim Kite was at physiotherapy, recuperating from a leg broken during the summer holidays, and I didn't bother asking for supply, partly because I'd rather save it for occasions when I haven't a chance to prepare anything, and partly because I'm still in the superstitious phase.

I'd noted a comment in a book I was reviewing (*In Tune with Yourself,* by Jennifer Dunn and others) to the effect that subjects for writing don't need searching for: they're all around us. The problem is focussing their minds . . .

Danielle's mother is Charlotte, the nursery teacher. Danielle wrote:

I hate having to get up in the morning because I have to get up at six o'clock in the morning to get to school because we have to clean our teeth and me [and] my brother take a long time doing it. I have to have my breakfast and I have rice crispies nearly every morning and so does my brother and my mum and dad have toast most times. Some mornings the room smells of bacon. Then I have to get dressed, getting my skirt and top on, socks and knickers and shoes on. Then I have to pack my bag. 'Lunch?' 'Yes' 'Book?' 'Yes' 'PE stuff?' 'Yes'. 'Get in the car' says mum. 'Yes Mum' I say. Then we're at the nursery. I put out the shop and the playhouse, setting the things on the shelves and things. 'Now it's time to go to school' 'OK'. I'm standing on the playground. It is cold. Time to go in and start work.

I sent this to Charlotte, who sent a note back to her daughter: 'What about the bit when I burst into tears and BEG you to hurry up?'

Simon is in the same class. He is very small and extremely shortsighted, and has been ringingly identified by his mother as dyslexic: 'I was dyslexic, his sister is and he is and I want something done about it before it's too late.' He wrote on mornings: 'I don't like getting up. My brother pours some water on my bed. The water soaks through my bed. Then I have my breakfast.' My comment on his book, I noted much later, is 'Oh dear. Lovely.'

While most of the children were writing, six were painting. I found the computer in the classroom's adjacent quiet room, and set two children off on a program called MOSAIC, experimenting with colour patterns. So by 9.45 I had the sort of classroom I like: three activities going on, not too much spelling to correct because not everyone's writing, and a dramatic elephant taking shape under Alice's brush. 'This', she said, 'is my favourite television programme, 'Around the World in Eighty Days with Phineas Fogg'.

Illustration 1: The Secretary in Her Office

From my notes:

> 7 January. Kate [health visitor] rang to find out whether Ben Andrews
> can get early entry to the nursery. It has to go through the office but
> the answer's almost certainly yes because Ben's big brother Justin is ill
> with a brain tumour and Mrs A is pregnant. J comes to school
> part-time. 'The prognosis isn't good', says Kate.

The Andrews had taken Justin to Disneyland last term, and I'd assumed things
were bad. We all think of our children at home. But Justin is still around,
wearing a white skull cap to disguise the loss of his hair because of the
radiotherapy. His teacher, Janice, says he is becoming a little forgetful, but
that most of his work is excellent.

This year the weather crisis didn't occur. Very little snow fell, and school got
going much as normal every day. The unseasonal warmth led to minor
infections, but at least there was nothing like last year's icy roads; teachers
blocked away from school by two-foot drifts, and terror-striking broadcasts by
local radio; or trees knocked across roads by October's hurricane, that everybody
knew about except Dawn, Daniel and I. The next morning Charlotte thought I
was joking: 'You mean you slept through that?' I'd driven to school,
negotiating huge fallen trees, mounting grass verges, to find the LEA had
closed schools on local radio. Four children had walked half a mile through the
furious winds, unaccompanied. Even Stuart had closed over at Watercombe
Junior, and normally he is like the Windmill: the show goes on whatever.

I sometimes wonder what my reputation is like among the parents. There are
those, of course, in Cowper Drive itself, who send their children to Edinburgh
Road because of me. A woman said last year, 'Do you realise how sarcastic you
are?' I hadn't thought I was. A man had said it was all right for his wife to lose
her temper, but not for me: 'She's only a stupid woman, you're a headmaster.'
He was half-right, of course. He also said, at a parents' evening: 'I'm here under
duress, of course. Mandy made me come. I think parents should stay out of
school. I think there should be some mystery about education, all this parents
can come in when they want to, I don't like it . . .'

Some parents think I'm too heavy with children who bully others.
Dyslexic Simon (mother's diagnosis, not mine) was brought to me with blood
still dripping from his forehead, and when the dinner lady took the tissue
briefly away, I could see a bit of his skull. I phoned home, and unusually, was
able to get both parents with one call: Father is on nights. They arrived at
school, Mother smoking nervously. As I did not have my car at school, I'd
called a taxi, which was now ticking over in the car park. 'Emergency is it?' said
the driver. 'OK'. A sticker on the window said 'NO SMOKING'.

I found two boys, Damien and Mark, had been fighting; had been told to

stop; had gone on — and had eventually pushed bystander Simon off the wall
and 'his glasses went into his head', as Mark put it. I found those glasses later,
like a Hitchcock emblem, fresh blood still on the lenses. The boys admitted
their part in it when I shocked them by describing Simon's injury.

> I am sorry to have to tell you that —————— was involved in some
> fighting today which led to a serious accident. As this is by no means
> the first occasion when —————— has disobeyed a member of my staff
> and carried on fighting, I must ask you to keep him at home at
> lunchtimes until further notice.

Simon is a pale 8-year-old, small and thin for his age. He is also short-sighted,
and his glasses are pebbly and important. He once said to me at 10.00 am, 'Is it
dinner time yet?' He has no confidence in himself and writes his painstakingly
acquired letters with the help of the special needs teacher, a vocabulary book,
help from friends on his table and Tim Kite: 'What's your problem, Simon?'

Actually, it was a bit of the wall that went into Simon's head. He was
released from hospital the same day, but vomited through the night, and was
re-admitted in the morning. I took assembly and told the children — juniors
only — about Simon: about the bone showing. Then I told the story of Daniel
in the lions' den. As I got back from assembly, Damien's father rang. I quote
my notes, made immediately:

> Mr A rang. Claimed Damien was innocent. I said I trusted the dinner
> lady who had seen the incident, and that there was a 'background' of
> Damien fighting. 'You mean he's got a reputation? I've seen this before
> when I was an NCO. One bloke's got a reputation for trouble and
> whenever he's near anything, he gets it.' I said I had seen Damien
> fighting. 'Look, When Damien gets hit, I tell him, "Deck 'em".
> 'Well, there's a conflict between what you teach your son and what we
> do.' He turned to Damien, So I could still hear him, but less clearly.
> 'Look. From now on, you talk to nobody. Nobody. Get that?' Back,
> direct to the mouthpiece: 'There. I've solved that for you . . .'

A week later, Mark's grandfather came to see me. He is a powerful man of 60 or
so, still working for British Rail. I was almost certain I'd stood next to him on
the Falcon terrace at the City ground. He was burning with injustice about how
I'd treated Mark, and dropped dark hints about legal advice. I explained that
Mark had been caught fighting many times, and that this was the last straw.
Did he know about other times when I'd spoken to . . . was it his daughter?
. . . 'Stepdaughter. No. I didn't know about them. But Mark said you
wouldn't listen when he tried to explain ...'

There's truth in this. We find dogs to give bad names to, and hang them.
And Mark has a terrible name. Now he won't come to school for any part of the
day. When his grandfather tried to get me to lift the lunchtime ban, I saw
Simon's skull briefly . . . and said, 'No. But if Mark attends for a week, going
home at lunchtimes, and not getting into trouble at other times, Damien and

he can come back to school dinners next Friday . . .' Mark's grandfather agreed to these terms, and offered his number at BR in case of trouble. We were about to part as near-friends, fellow City supporters, 'blunt straightforward Englishmen' who've had their say, and who've no cause to rail, or cry, or snivel — oh, how well we chaps arrange these things when there aren't any women around! — when I asked him about home — he'd hinted it might be a reason for Mark's violence:

> It's a maisonette I've got . . . There's the wife, her two daughters and their kids, one each, and my stepson, his marriage has broken up, his kid, all under one roof . . . When you get a ready-made family, you get people who aren't your kind, I'll be frank with you . . . they're all under one roof. Mark's like a wild bull when he's released, I can tell you, he's like a caged animal . . .

That's eight humans in a tiny house. Anyway, I said I'd let the boys in next Friday. The dinner ladies had commented how much easier things were on the playground since Damien and Mark had been going home for lunch (or, in Mark's case, not coming to school at all). There'd be little sympathy in that quarter for children living in tiny rented accommodation, roughing up pur-blind duffers like Simon.

A teacher showed me his record book:

> Just spent the evening reading a book of children's poems after working at school till 6.00. Can I now justify the time to write up my record book? It is useful to reflect on the day and in many ways this book is just a series of random thoughts as they occur. True they chronicle major events in the day but they do not set out a plan or formal journal of all that has been covered. But then how can they? I cannot hope to record all that has been taught or all that each child has experienced in a day. (So what good are record sheets?) What I can hope to do is to try and give a texture to the atmosphere within the area (classroom) and the type of experience we give the children.
>
> Have moved Jennifer up a colour on her reading and she is thrilled — a gamble but seems to have paid off. M and C seem happier after a period treading water and at times getting under . . .

Margaret (10 years old) comes to see me, sobbing. 'They're going to say I kicked Graham, and I did, but only because he said I was a nigger, Mr Sedgwick . . .' Slowly she calms down in my room with a book, while I make some phone calls. She is dressed in a flimsy blouse and skirt, and short socks.

I visited a school in another authority to do an in-service session on children's writing. When I got there, I was dying for the loo, anxious to find out where I was to set up my stall, and in need of a cup of tea.

> I'm sure you'd like a look round my school. I went on a management course. It was brought in, not just education . . . It was very good, very slick. He knew how to use a video . . .
> My display girl puts these up. She tells the other teachers the sizes things have to be, and within that they have complete freedom. She's wizard at art and craft . . .'

The expenses form cheered me up and the talk went satisfactorily: the story (I'll tell it in Chapter 6) about *The Sun's* editorial often breaks the ice. (The cheque will cheer me up even more!) While I was there, the deputy at Cowper was running a staff meeting. Here are some extracts from Sue's notes of this meeting:

1   The remaining two Baker days are to be split and used hourly. First hour is on Thursday 21 January at 3.45, to discuss INSET on 16 February.
2   INSET — 16 February — 4.00-6.00 'Hey Mr Tambourine Man': music for us, Edinburgh Road and Valley School.
3   Janice suggested we base Spring concert on music INSET.
4   2nd Baker hour is 28 January after school to discuss and sort storage of instruments and music materials.
5   Maths evening for parents 24 March to be discussed more fully at next staff meeting . . .
6   Playground duty — indoor play — junior teachers to include on their patrol the two infant classes now included in the junior area.
7   Dates:
14 Jan. Peggy Baker visiting from Eastyorkgate.
19 Jan. Jim Raines — advisory teacher for computers 3.45-6.00.
21 Jan. Visitors from Sorbringworth to see children's writing at Cowper.
25 Jan. infant disco at 12.00.
26 Jan. PTA Committee meeting 7.30.
28 Jan. Kenny Roberts (county library) working with Barbara, lunch-hour.
1 Feb. Iris starts jury service: supply (if any) arranged day by day.
2 Feb. FS out all day as visiting writer at Sorbringworth: we have supply, and it will be used for Lynda to help with music in Donna's and Jeanette's.
3 Feb. Staff meeting.
4 Feb. Junior Disco at 12.00.
8 Feb. Mixed disco at 12.00 (all these discos for school funds).
9 Feb. Book group after school.

10 Feb. Mobile Library in morning.
16 Feb. Music INSET evening.
18 Feb. FS at Sorbringworth again — supply arrangements as before.
19 Feb. Civvies Day: theme to be decided [this is a day when staff and children may wear what they like, contributing 20p each to school funds].
19 Feb. Governors' meeting.

I watch most mornings to see if Justin is in. He is today, and he does me a careful drawing of a yucca plant, which his mother admires. She has a hospital appointment this afternoon, whether for her or for Justin I don't know. I watch her go. I don't understand her courage.

Fiona, a 6-year-old Jehovah's Witness, looks at us all with contempt. But it's understandable: if mum and dad say that all we tell you about God is rubbish, how can she not believe everything else is rubbish too? God was Man in Palestine? Junk. Don't run with those scissors, Fiona . . .

In Mrs Thatchers pocket there is Kenneth Bakers cane, arthur scargills mining drill, part of raguns nose that got chopped off in a confrence meeting, deneses townail clippings, a chued ticket to the odeun, a torn uann Jack flag, the key to 10 downing street rapped in muchy pease, one of neil kinnocks remaining heirs. ps She has got big pockets

As I typed it up, 10-year-old Christopher's piece looked like this:

In Mrs Thatcher's pocket there is
Kenneth Baker's cane
Arthur Scargill's mining drill
part of Reagan's nose that got chopped off in a conference meeting
Denis's toe-nail clippings
a chewed ticket to the Odeon
a torn Union Jack flag
the key to 10 Downing Street wrapped in mushy peas
one of Neil Kinnock's remaining hairs.
p.s. She has got big pockets.

On my 43rd birthday, a lecturer from Trent Polytechnic rang to congratulate me on an article I'd published in *The Times Educational Supplement* on the National Curriculum, the insecure place of the arts in it, and the link between them — which is, I'd argued, the gradual crumbling of democracy. But it quickly emerged he had another reason for ringing. He hadn't seen the piece till a colleague had sent a copy of it across to him with a note attached: 'Fred Sedgwick lives!'

The Poly has a fictional group of schools, the Bonsall Campus, which they use to set problems for the education students. Peter Shirley, the lecturer, went on, 'The head of the secondary is very go-ahead, wants to make his school better, wants to improve things for everyone. His main opponent is the primary head, who is ready to retire, and who dreads the phone ringing every morning. The thing is, the primary head's name is . . . Fred Sedgwick!'

We savoured coincidences for a minute or two. He didn't offer me money to go up to Trent Poly to talk to the students as the real FS who was go-ahead and energetic (but who, nevertheless, dreaded the phone ringing every morning). Two days later I received a letter from Peter, accompanied by a file of excellent material. It turns out they call him 'Frederick Sedgwick'. 'Sounds like a speech impediment', said Cowper's deputy:

> Dear Fred,
>
> Enclosed as promised a copy of the Bonsall Campus Folder and the kind of problems which our students are prepared to tackle as part of their 4th year work in Education Studies. We use case studies and problem solving to try to develop professional skills.
>
> It is an enormous coincidence that we should have chosen your name for the Head of this imaginary primary school.
>
> As we suggested on the telephone we will have to write him out of the simulation — we will either have him slip into the threshing machine as they did in 'The Archers', or perhaps it would be more fitting after long service in present day schools to give him a pools win of a few hundred thousand and ship him off to an early retirement in Majorca!
>
> I look forward to reading more of your occasional articles in the TES, although I hope we have no more coincidences of this sort.
> Best Wishes,
>
> Peter Shirley (Education Studies Co-ordinator)

Sue noticed that Simon had a wart on his finger that, like O'Connell street in Dublin, had its natural proportions reversed. O'Connell Street is broader than it is long, while Simon's wart was longer than it was broad. Simon had told Sue that the GP had said there was nothing she could do about it. I phoned School Health, and the schools' doctor came up and wrote letters to the GP and the hospital. 'There's two schools of thought about warts — treat 'em or don't treat 'em' . . .

A head from another authority at an INSET meeting after school one day:

> The word 'shrewd' is interesting as used about successful educational
> officers: it means they don't say anything, they sit on the fence . . . I've
> got total contempt for them . . . one of them said to me, 'You ought to
> watch out Compton, you're getting a reputation as a Bolshie bastard
> . . .' I've stayed in the union, I've got no time for their lackeys' union,
> their bloody NAHT, and I've no time for the managerial cant about
> teacher appraisal . . . I don't care who appraises me, the caretaker, the
> crossing patrol lady, as long as it isn't one of those fence-sitters who
> wouldn't recognise education if it kicked them up the bum . . .

Many of the pressures on teachers in 1988 were new, because of GRIST (Grant-
Related In-Service Training), a system that forced us to negotiate training needs
inside a pyramid of schools, topped by the local high; and, in fact, to design
much of that training ourselves. It was interesting, some cynics noted, that
education — that regenerative concept — was not mentioned in these schemes:
it was always training.

'A semantic quibble?' queried my chairman. No, training's about riding a
bike, typing, the breast-stroke, putting up wallpaper, washing up, cracking
the code of the Amstrad PCW system. Education's about becoming 'freer and
more creative' with science, or the arts, or the humanities.

In any event, the staff meeting notes recorded above were about teachers
planning:

a music INSET for the three local primaries,
an action plan following the review,
a parents' maths evening,
a meeting to talk about new LEA maths testing,
an in-school INSET arising from me being out of the school as a writer,
dance INSET in the pyramid,
initiatives from Janice's and Barbara's attendance on a course on
whole-school aproaches,
other meetings arranged voluntarily, in the old-fashioned way, by teachers
with passions for children's literature for example, or dance, or poetry . . .

This last kind of meeting, common in the past, is disappearing, as so many
compulsory (or 'Baker') meetings suck on the profession's time.

This contradicts the NAHT view of the state of things: it isn't just the
heads who are under pressure, it's the whole profession. The gross new
statutoriness, on the one hand, and the sense teachers have of the needs to
educate themselves — as well as the children — on the other, are in conflict.
The strains in this might crack us. But in the year 2000, I want to be among
the teachers who negotiated the Philistine years with my spirit unbroken.

Lynda told me, 'I've applied for an artistic post at the Birmingham Hippodrome.' She asked me to look through her letter with a view to making it stronger. I crossed out 'fun' and replaced it with 'rewarding'.

I've got a horrible and wicked teacher. If I'm ever late for school I have to do 100 lines. Or I have to stand outside in the rain if it's raining. This is what happened to me the other day. I was on my bike on my way to school when I crashed into a brick wall outside school and my teacher came out with the class and he said 'You're late, and look at your front wheel, it's buckled.' I felt like being cheeky, so I said 'Wouldn't yours be?' He sent me inside to write 'I must not be cheeky' a hundred times.
When I had finished I had to fix my bike.
When I had done it I had to go into dinner.
After dinner my teacher banged into the school wall. I walked up to him and said 'Look at your wheel. Would you like to go in and do a hundred lines or stay out in the rain?' He looked as if he would burst but he didn't. The headmaster was looking out of a window. He looked at me and laughed.

Sarah (10) showed me that the Beano is still influential in its portrayal of teachers . . . but her subversive nerve is something teachers might need in the future.

At the School Disco

Play the record mister
play it very loud   so
I can hear the rhythm thump
against the dancing crowd

Play it so the words drive
hard into my head   so
I can sing them to myself
when I'm safe in bed

Play it so that Clare and I
can forget our cares   and
catch that melody and noise
and love them unawares

Sarah doesn't come to the discos we run to raise money for the school funds. They pretend to no other status than a fund-raising event, and the children are charged 20p for entry, and 10p for a glass of coke or lemonade.

We play a tape prepared by Gillian (who doubles as a disc jockey for local Hospital Radio) as loudly as the school equipment permits — which is not nearly as loudly as Craig's teenage brother can play his records in his bedroom opposite my room. The disco takes place in the PE dome, a separate building next to the swimming pool. Some of the children arrive at school on disco mornings in civvies, ranging from old-fashioned party wear to trendy clothes from soap opera and 'Top of the Pops'. The boys, however, are mostly in Cowper jumpers and grey trousers. They often begin by belting round the room in lines, arms round each other's shoulders. We stop this after a moment or two and get everyone either dancing, or making an attempt at it; 6-year-old girls, facing each other, waggle their hips, while 9- and 10-year-olds arrange themselves in groups, and teach each other new dances.

Pauline and Danielle (Clare in the poem) love disco-dancing, though I suspect our lunchtime sessions are tame compared with what's going on in their heads, as they jiggle hips, touch right elbow with left hand, waving right hand in the air; all the while miming the words. When I pointed them out to Danielle's mother, she commented, 'No worse than shouting at a football match.'

Traditional fund-raising events don't always work well at Cowper, and three of these affairs can bring in about £70. If we add to this the £250 commission from the firm that takes the photographs of the children, we have the school fund's main source of revenue. The PTA funds are another, though not very different story. Things will be bad round here when we have to go cut-throatedly private. This is no doubt on the agenda for the next ten years.

I wrote to Emmanuel Jegede:

> We are looking forward to your residency at Cowper next term. Perhaps you could write to me soon or give me a ring to discuss arrangements? The following days would be fine with me — could you choose the one that suits you and let me know.
>
> We are greatly looking forward to your time with us.
>
> Yours sincerely

This was a project planned with GRIST money. With help from Liz Tagg of the local Arts Association (which was paying his fees) we had discovered in catalogues, slides and photographs Emmanuel Taiwo Jegede, a Yoruba painter, sculptor, poet and musician, who was going to spend seven days in the school in March, working with Lynda's class of lower juniors. The main planning for this had happened way back in December, and I was getting worried.

Sally, the nursery nurse, asked me if she could leave thirty minutes early on

Illustration 2: The Birch Tree

Friday week to go to a NALGO conference. She wanted to get other nursery nurses together, using the auspices of the union. But another nurse said to Dawn, my wife, who was teaching in another nursery, 'I don't mind getting together as long as it doesn't become political.' You might as well say, I don't mind going for a walk as long as I don't have to breathe in air.

A member of a primary in-service planning group, meeting at 5.00 at the teachers' centre, told us that he's not at liberty to inform us of what he knows, but, by golly, if he was we'd be surprised. If only he could speak freely! I got up, pulled him out of his chair by his armpits, kneed him in the groin twice, and then, as he staggered about the room folded in two, brought my fists down heavily and repeatedly on to the back of his neck, accompanying his fall with what Kingsley Amis once described as 'a brief manic flurry of obscene gestures'. Nobody made any attempt to stop me.

I exaggerate slightly here. What happened was, I left the meeting at 6.30, had a swift half at The Dog, and went home. Wrote that last paragraph.

Phone call: 'Jerry, you haven't sent me that reference.' 'Sorry mate, I'll send it today.'

Mrs Harriet Larkin
Harriet Larkin has worked at this school as a supply teacher. I have found her to be reliable in all that she is asked to do. Her work appears to be well prepared and she has a sympathetic attitude towards the children.
Yours

Phone call:
Me: Cowper School. Good Morning.
Caller: Have you an accompanist in school?
Me: No, who's calling?
Caller: Thank you, goodbye.
Phone call (same day):
Me: Cowper School. Good Morning.
Caller: Do you have any vacancies on your dinner lady reserve list?
Me: Yes. Can I have your name please?
Caller: Because you've only got one, haven't you?
Me: May I have your name, please?
Caller: Never mind about that now. You *have* only got one, haven't you?
Me: I can't put your name on the list if I haven't got it —
Caller: Forget about it. [Hangs up]

Phone call: Shaun Waller's mum says the dinner ladies are bullying him.

If I was a teacher I would tell the children what to do, and tell them to put their chairs on the table (Selina, 5)

I would tell people off if they spit (Neil, 6)

I would be Mr Sedgwick and send children to my office if they are naughty (Junior, 6)

I would let the children chalk if they are good (Leanne, 5)

I would tidy up and hang lots of pretty pictures (Carla, 6)

I would paint pictures of Roger Red-hat all the time and help the children to read (James, 5)

I would not tell children off if they are naughty (Andrew, 5)

I would be lazy in the staffroom all day and let the children go in the bushes (Daniel, 6)

There'd been a coup d'état last October, when, at the end of the Parent Teacher Association's annual general meeting, a parent I'd never got on with nominated the deputy for the post of chairman. Conventionally at Cowper, the head had always retained this role, probably to prevent any surreptitious snaffling of power by the parents, who, one is always being told, only want the basic skills for their children, and who would distort the curriculum if they had control over the buying policy. I had kept this arrangement through inertia and something like instinct, using the AGM to make points about government action and its effect on the life of the children and teachers in the school. Rather piously, I suppose now, I'd always tried to insist on the primacy of education in the school, over fund-raising, for example, and public relations. Raising money in my spare time while successive secretaries of state remove it while I'm working adds a new dimension to the word 'thankless'.

The deputy was always less doctrinaire than I am, although he too hated seeing teachers behind chuck-a-sponge games on rainy Sundays in the summer. Anyway, I won't forget his embarrassed look when Mrs Skinner nominated him out of the blue. 'Advice, Headmaster?' he asked in the tone of voice we both used with each other, mimicking public school styles. On this occasion I couldn't respond in kind. I was fed up by what I saw as an insult.

But I soon learned to live with the happy consequences of this decision: the deputy took on all the routine problems of PT relations. He was better at it than I, having an eye for detail and a conciliatory charm that I lack. Though, at the first meeting he chaired — before he led the planning of a coffee morning to take place after a concert the children and staff were preparing — he slapped down a group at the end of the table who were holding a private conversation: 'Could we concentrate on the matter in hand, please?' He quietly tolerated my points about the probable effects of the privatization of cleaning and catering.

He came across, I think, as a much nicer chap than me. I swore to myself never to be a chairman of a PTA again . . .

Mrs Andrews has had her baby, a girl, Faye. She brought her into the nursery today with Ben and Justin and we admired her, cocooned against the weather by polythene. Justin's hair has grown again, after the radiotherapy, and he is doing well in school.

Near us, 4½-year-old Junior watched intently as Tim Kite, in the nursery for just this purpose during the lunch-hour, expertly holed a coconut. ('Twice, or the milk won't come out', he explained to Charlotte.) Junior, watching every movement of Tim's hand, unwittingly demonstrated how daft it is to talk about 'injecting enthusiasm for learning into small children', as a writer in a magazine for teachers did recently. The enthusiasm is palpably there, obvious to anyone but the most boorish basic-skilling Philistine. What schools do sometimes, and I do not exclude my own teaching from this damning stricture, is to find the rough position of the enthusiasm the child has come in with, and suck it out. 'I've brought this shell in Mr —.' 'Sit down, please, Sarah, while I do the register.' 'Putting ticks in a little row' (as Allan Ahlberg sums up a teacher's admin tasks, in *Please Mrs Butler*) is all too often more interesting than Sarah's shell; Lesley's birthday, which is one day nearer now, but still a week away; even Charlene's grandad's death.

Mrs Waller, who said the dinner ladies were bullying her son Shaun, complained to me that when I told him off in her presence I'd placed my hand on his shoulder. 'I didn't like that . . . I didn't like that at all.' This followed my complaining about Shaun's putting his hands between girls' thighs, following, in turn, other parents' complaints about that.

Later, Grandma came in. She's less aggressive than her daughter. 'I can't understand why Shaun's like he is — we tell him stories about Jesus . . . We tell him to be a good boy.'

These were the recommendations of the review, on which the staff were asked to act — first, by preparing a response:

> Job descriptions for all staff should be modified and completed . . . the school should review the allocation of posts of responsibility . . . There should be further development within the context of the school of (a) how children learn (b) the quality of children's learning (c) equipment and resources (d) the allocation of expenditure . . . The school's record-keeping system should be reviewed . . . The school should extend the support to children with special educational needs across a wider range of curriculum activities . . . There should be a review of the use of PE storage space . . .

Some heads write school curriculum papers, and responses to LEA initiatives, themselves. I didn't want to do that, partly because the resulting document would be useless: having had no stake in its creation, the staff would not have read it; and also, I simply didn't want the job of writing institutionalized prose on my own for a market that didn't exist. The alternative is the liberal management one: get the teachers to write it themselves. If it's their school, get them to make up policy. There's a beguiling reductio ad absurdem hanging around here: liberals believe the school belongs to the children. The Plowden Report was subtitled *Children and Their Primary Schools*. Why not get the kids to write all this stuff . . .?

Of course, the liberal management line is seductive. But there are two problems. The first, which used to concern me greatly in my first years in headship, is the risk that a sub-committee of teachers might hijack the school away from my chosen path. I might, in other words, be left at the helm of a ship that had restored Beta Maths, or the Ladybird reading scheme ('because it's cheap and it works', as a head said to me in 1977), not to mention housepoints and smacking. This worry faded as I realized that I wasn't so sure of the right path as I had been and that most teachers don't want this kind of power, because it takes time and brings about responsibility.

The more adhesive anxiety about liberal management is that committee formation is a mode not of power devolvement, as its rhetoric suggests, but of control. Heads are constantly complaining that their time is being taken up with the reading and writing of memos, reports, consultation documents, discussion papers and so on: those 'useless bits of paper' that Charles Causley identifies in his poem 'School at Four O'Clock.'

Now 'consultation document' has a democratic ring. But the periods given for responses are often comically short: in the case of the National Curriculum papers, for example. And when heads are meeting to form those responses, they are not educating anyone: not the children, not their colleagues back in school, not themselves. They aren't helping anyone to become an autonomous decision-maker who will, by the example and practice of that decision-making, be more able in years to come to live creatively and efficiently in a semi-democratic society.

What is happening in these times of responding, reading, drafting, re-drafting, writing, phoning is that the heads are being controlled. The more paper, the less real life. The more meetings (often about meetings), the more chance of power staying where it is: at the top of the monolith. As heads, we control teachers when we make them meet to form policy that will largely be ignored anyway. Liberal management is really a benign control system.

Nevertheless, I asked two probationary teachers and the nursery teacher to help me draft the response to the LEA's demands. The four of us met at our house, and this is part of what we wrote:

> We feel that 'how children learn' should be seen in the wider context of how *people* learn; in other words, of how *we* learn . . . a good school is composed of learning adults as well as learning children . . .

There has already been much productive discussion of equipment and resources with regard to music and mathematics, and the resulting rationalisation has led to greater efficiency and better learning for the children . . .

Children should be taught to use stock responsibly and well, and they should be constantly aware of all that is available to them . . .

The record system falls into two parts:

1) We should continue to make forecasts available to all colleagues at the beginning of each half term. Teachers should be responsible for checking areas covered in previous classes. It should be noted that the school's excellent display already ensures that there is plenty of information available of this kind . . .

2) Individual children's records . . . should recognise that learning does not occur in a linear way; that it can be haphazard at its best; that checklists of 'experiences' are useless. More importantly, moralising or personal statements are unprofessional . . .

It will be noted that these recommendations require extra resources, and we look forward to hearing about these allocations.

There is some show of spirit here: the mention of resources at the end, for example, and the unfashionable insistence that 'quality' is not an objective reality, nor learning a tidy system that will be readily subsumed into targets.

A long half is coming to an end. During a staff meeting a teacher, Janice, wonders if, in addition to the two meetings coming up to plan INSET on maths and political education, there shouldn't be a 'feedback' session on an earlier maths afternoon. 'No', I say, and mumble something about meetings about meetings about meetings. Afterwards Tim tells a joke, complete with stage Italian accent:

Jesus comes back to earth and lands up in the Vatican. Two priests say, 'Jesus has returned! We'd better tell someone!' So they tell two monsignores, who go to the cardinal: 'Jesus has come back! He's in St Peter's!' The cardinals go to the Pope: 'Papa, Papa, Jesus has come back to earth! He's in St Peter's!' And the Pope replies: 'I know. Get your heads down, look busy . . .'

As assembly ended on the Monday morning of the last week, Sue the secretary came to tell me, 'Stuart is on the phone.' Stuart has been my friend since we both fell about when another head on our induction course referred to his school's 'infrastructure'. We have planned applications for jobs together over pints of beer (for him, draft Guinness laced with blackcurrant, so that the creamy head looks as though you've cut your finger into it). Stuart had been working, expenses only, as a football scout — first for Watford, then for Aston Villa. And now . . .

Hello Stuart.
Are you sitting down?
Yes.
I've resigned.
Bloody hell.
[silence]
I'm going to Watford.
What as?
Chief Scout —
That's great!
— and Youth Development Officer. I'm going Friday.
Bloody hell.
Quite.

On the last day, Emmanuel Jegede spent an hour with us planning his residency. Tim led a delightful concert for parents. But apart from these happy events, that Friday was a disaster: a row with a parent before school, another complaining that her 11-year-old daughter does too much formal maths and English, and 'not enough exciting work, like she's had in every other year in this school'; Christopher Thorn was taken to hospital with a cut on the back of his head (one stitch); and in the governors' meeting, the chairman insisted that the distinction between 'training' and 'education' was 'merely semantic'. And then, that fight.

While I was back at the table with my minutes, a constable came. The child-minder had told him how she'd gone out for a drink with the other woman's husband, who'd often beaten his wife up. The wife had spent time in the women's refuge, and she'd gone there now. I wondered, idly, over my agenda, who'd be bringing the children in the following week. I remembered Christina's wide eyes as I led her mother away.

The last professional act of the term was to go to Stuart's leaving do after school on that disastrous Friday. I stayed for an hour, then walked the two miles home in the cold, pre-spring air. I thought of him with new, sudden problems. Moving house with his wife and three children into an expensive area. Finding new players on the common on dull Sunday mornings. Worrying about a three-and-a-half-year contract. And I thought, Lucky Sod.

Chapter 2

No Problem (March)

> I was a flower, a blossoming flower,
> Plucked from the bush by Olabisi . . .
> (Emmanuel Jegede)

Peotry is sissy stuff that rhymes . . . Aktually there is only one piece of peotry in the english language:

> i come from haunts of coot and hern
> i make a sudden sally
> and er-hem-er-hem-er-hem the fern
> to bicker down a valley
> (Willans and Searle)

Art is not a handicraft, it is a transmission of feeling the artist has experienced. (Tolstoy, *What Is Art?*)

I sent an early draft of that to my editor, Geoff, and he commented that it did not catch enough of the essential scrappiness of the job. 'The good news, Fred — and remember this when I've said the rest — is that it's OK, fine . . . but could you catch that sense of things happening all together . . . often, in a headship, you don't know which way to turn, do you? . . . could you get that feeling in places? . . .'

There are problems in recording this hurly-burly, this shambles, this unsystematic multiple collision of human possibilities. One is to ensure the absence of a whingeing tone when the going gets tough. A more important problem is that, while you're being pulled in five directions, you're in no position to lumber yourself with a sixth (if one can be lumbered with a direction) that's telling you, Get this down. Get it down. Now, before you forget. You might as well ask a goalkeeper who's watching a finely weighted cross and three rushing strikers while conscious of his full-back lying on the ground, to listen to the advice of a man in the crowd behind the goal; all the while mentally recording the event for his report in the football paper.

It is inevitable that much of this material is lost, and the rest recorded later when the tension is gone: commotion recollected in tranquillity. Nevertheless, here is a morning in late winter: scrappy, worrying, as much as it felt as possible. But even this leaves out conversations and events that didn't seem significant at the time, but which turned out to be important. Even this is tidied up. It begins just after assembly . . .

Charlotte tells me Jenny's grandad has died, and she is going to the funeral. 'It'll be just like assembly', Jenny says.

Lynda and I talk about the artist coming later this half: everything seems to be ready.

We've advertised a summer reception job, for that large intake of children at Easter. Mrs Punton-Browne, a candidate, calls, after making an appointment, and when I get back from assembly and my talk with Lynda about Emmanuel Jegede, she and her 3-year-old son have been waiting ten minutes in my room. Sue tells me later that during that time mother and son did not say a word to each other. Amongst other things, I ask Mrs Punton-Browne, 'And where is your daughter at school?' 'At the convent — she couldn't take the bustle of Camden Road . . . she's very shy.' I show her around, and as she leaves, another candidate arrives, this time without an appointment, and I show her round too. 'Is anyone applying that you already know?' 'Yes. But it's not fixed.' 'I don't want to bother if you got someone in mind.' 'It's not fixed.' Then another candidate rings, under the false impression, caused by a clerical error between us and the office, that the post is permanent.

I set two 10-year-olds going on the new RM Nimbus computer in the library: a program called ART. You use a handheld 'mouse' to draw and colour a picture on a screen. They pick up the idea very quickly and I leave them to it. 'I'll be in my room if you want any help.'

During coffee I photocopy a set of poems teachers have written following a course I'd led one Saturday in January at the LEA's residential centre. I get them ready to be sent out in cyclostyled booklets. The staff sit drinking coffee, and discussing problems: not usually children, but declining resources. We are out of yellow and white paint. I note that we are in a no smoking zone except for Sue, the secretary.

The PE adviser calls to look at the hall floor, which is becoming unsuitable for barefoot work. We want it recovered, but apparently this is very expensive. The adviser comments that the floor has been mistreated by successive caretakers, and we both note craters made by high-heeled shoes: another reason for not having any more PTA dances! 'This job has to go through Education, not Cleaning and Maintenance', says the adviser. 'I'll do it.' Great — a job I can forget about. We gossip for five minutes about the internal politics of the society's officers and advisers. She hasn't heard from Stuart, and I tell her about Watford's results: not good.

I change the computer children for two others, leaving the first pair to induct the second in the ways of the program. There are several techniques of drawing and shading available to the children. I admire the program because, unlike most others, it gives the children control over the screen: they can make a design that's never been made before. Most of the early software was no more than electronic Ladybird stuff. The caretaker walks by. I tell him about the floor. He looks at the Nimbus screen: 'School's so much more interesting than it was in my day.'

I teach for an hour, some close observation of stuffed animals: a snake, a frog, a badger, a fox, a shrew. This leads to writing and drawing. Perhaps this sort of work is becoming a cliché at Cowper, but it has a calming effect on the children. In the silence one can almost hear the learning going on: about the animals, about the nature of learning, about their materials: pencils, words, crayons . . . Margaret is quiet and her tongue protrudes slightly in her effortless concentration.

A rep calls with a wooden building system that would work wonders for CDT from nursery to top juniors, and which, like the Nimbus program ART, would give the children an autonomy of sorts over their materials.

> 'I'm convinced. How much is it?'
> 'We also supply a set of workcards an adviser in ————shire has written for us'
> 'How much is it?'
> 'It is excellent for developing imaginatory [*sic*] play'
> 'How much?'
> 'I can see I can't keep you in suspense any longer. With everything you need to use the workcards, and to get the full educational benefit from the package, you're talking about, well, less than £300.'
> 'How much less?'
> 'It's £298.'
> 'Forget it, I can't afford it.'

> Stella has trouble swallowing grated carrot — Julie has to cut it up for her, and it often falls out of her mouth! Today she ate a lettuce leaf, two pieces of cucumber. She comments to the other children that chips are fattening. When she puts her nightie on, her sister says that she [Stella] is getting fat.

This is a note from the dinner ladies about an 11-year-old. I promise to get in touch with mother.

Three calls: all enrolling children in our nursery. The office rings because a parent is complaining that his son will only get one term while other children will get two, three even four. It's true: children with language problems, or an agoraphobic single parent — to take two examples — are offered early places by the admissions panel (advisory headteacher, adviser for pre-school special needs, and me, assisted by nursery teacher and Sue). And it's not possible to explain these cases to parents whose children are pushed back in the queue.

During one of these calls, 9-year-old George is sent to me by his teacher: 'I've had two pound coins stolen from my bag.' I look at him speechlessly. Body-search everyone? Ask for culprits to own up after an assembly on the eighth commandment? Make sure George actually had £2 (how)? Tell him off for having money in his bag? I continue looking at George speechlessly.

The morning is ending. Syreeta wants to go home to fetch her maths folder. This makes an impressive change from PE kit. 'You don't have to cross any roads, do you? . . . be careful . . .' I watch her go down the alley to her house, fifty yards away.

George reappears as I'm going to have lunch with the reception children: 'I've found that money — in my bag.' I remember the first rule of administration again: Don't do anything: you may not have to.

Cowper was being squeezed in the grip of the 'whole-school approach'. This followed last year's review, and a course Janice and Barbara had attended. Advisers assured me that this was essentially a methodological matter, a way of ensuring that children do not trip up against vastly different attitudes, both to knowledge and to themselves as humans. Indeed, we have all seen children — often our own — leave one teacher whose idea of writing was a daily copying from the blackboard from 9.30 to 10.00, to go to another who encouraged learning about the world, and the child's relationship to it, through 'the intolerable struggle with words and meanings', that is writing in the sense of composition making. We have seen similarly worrying effects in maths, PE and science.

Our whole-school approach had got under way by imposing a common theme. Charlotte had taken responsibility for what the LEA curriculum papers call, nounlessly, 'the social and political', and she had suggested that the school develop a newspaper theme for a week.

'I had an idea in bed last night and I've been dying to see if it would work.' Eight-year-old Caroline has been trying, on and off, for two days, to build a load-bearing table (the load being a telephone directory) using only newspaper and sellotape. These words, her first on arrival one morning, are, at the very least, a compliment to the task her teacher has set her.

Four classes have compiled their own newspapers, using pencil and paper: regrettably, we cannot afford the FRONT PAGE word processor program, which would have been useful this week. A lower junior class have taught themselves what Tim calls 'basic ransom note technique', cutting messages for each other from headlines. Danielle has received one that says, 'WATCH IT PRICEY I'M COMING FOR YOU', while Nichola has made a card to take home that says, 'DEAR MUMMY AND DADDY I LOVE YOU'.

Older children are turning over the pages of *The Guardian* and *The Sun*, comparing content, size of headline, sentence length, and use of photographs. Simone (11) holds up *The Sun*: 'This one says things that aren't all true.' Paul and Martyn compare reports of City's Saturday game in the local paper ('We were robbed') and a national ('Liverpool's cultured football was too much for their country cousins').

Charlotte commented that she'd had to censor some of the papers, which was a sign of the times, as well as a relevant issue itself. I asked her how she felt the week had gone:

> I felt pleased, didn't you? . . . It was a beginning (of work in the social and political area) and it went on past the week . . . there's some really good work been done . . . the variety's been impressive. I'd like to do something else next term, maybe on multicultural work: will that be OK? Maybe a Caribbean steel band . . . Donna and I have applied for that 'World in your classroom' course — you automatically get supply cover . . .

This is fine, of course. But with the new GRIST arrangements, and the paucity of teachers in the summer term — many of them have summer reception classes, or other work — finding cover is going to be the problem: we have been undertraining teachers for a long time. I've rung fifteen on occasions in the past, looking for supply cover:

'I'm working today.'
'I'd rather not.'
'I've got a dental appointment.'
'I haven't got anywhere for the children.'
'I'm seeing my friend today, and I have promised.'
'Oh no — I'm teaching fulltime now! Hasn't the office told you?'

Neither Mrs Punton-Browne nor the other candidate I showed round have applied for the part-time post.

It's his energy that strikes me . . . On a fast day he never stops working: 'It's all right when you get used to it.' I'd assumed, stereotyping, that this fasting was for a Muslim festival, but he tells me (over Kenco bags for me, nothing for him) it's for Lent.

He gives the children a piece of clay each and tells them to make an egg. I watch them roll the clay around in their hands, greatly enjoying the experience, giggling and relishing the sheer feel of the stuff. Then they put the eggs in a little pile; each child gets a glimpse of his or hers, and then, blindfold, they have to tell if the egg they're offered is their own . . . Lynda has not enjoyed this!

The second thing I notice about Emmanuel is his faith: in his art, in his techniques, in the children. They are strangers to him, but he trusts them: with his teaching, and with a beautiful ceramic bowl his catalogue prices at £850 . . .

Later in groups of three the children carve a polystyrene cube, 12" x 12", using knives borrowed from the kitchen and spokeshaves bought for the purpose. He asks them to choose a shape they fancy: a table with something on it: fruit, flowers, for example; or a man reading. Polystyrene crumbs are everywhere, like leprosy, or snow. This is Emmanuel on his first day in the school.

Other children were given a task to tell a story using clay, and Janice, in the infants, picked up this idea. Two very articulate 7-year-old girls made tiny models of a man, a snail, a cross, a hedge, a pond, and two houses. Then they told me the following story, moving the inch-high fragments of clay around:

> Once upon a time there was a man who lived in a house in a wood. One morning he woke up feeling strange. So he said to his mum 'What shall I do?' 'Go to the doctor's on Monday' she said. 'Can I go in the garden now?' he said. So he went in the garden. He saw a pool. He got in it. It was a whirlpool. It carried him away. He went to the doctor's. 'I can't cure that' said the doctor. So he went home singing (doodle-oodle-oo). Next morning he woke up with a snail body. He went to the doctor's. The doctor said, 'I can't cure that'. So he went home singing (doodle-oodle-oo). Next morning he woke up with a cross body. He went to the doctor's. And the doctor said, 'I can't cure that'. So he went home singing (doodle-oodle-oo). But by the time he got home he was dead. The end.

Emmanuel was small in stature, strong and springy and constantly on the move. His catalogue told me that he was 45 years old, that he had exhibited all over the world since 1968 (when, I reflected, I'd qualified Cert. Ed.) and that his work had appeared in public in London, Kingston Jamaica, Lagos and Aylesbury; and in private collections in Brazil, Canada, Curacao, Czechoslovakia, France, Ghana, India, Nigeria, Trinidad, the UK and the USA.

His accent was powerfully African, despite his having lived in England for twenty years, and a parent said to me at the end of the first day, 'Can you understand what he's saying?' 'Yes, and so can the children.' Later the same parent referred to a child's stepfather as 'that blackie'. There is no good reason for pretending that these views, or feelings, or whatever they are, don't exist; and Cowper began to confront them because of Emmanuel Jegede's presence.

Emmanual tended to make life easier with a phrase that sounded sentimental when I first heard it, but which later came to reassure me: 'Emmanuel, could you spend some time with the nursery?' 'No problem.' 'Can we put on an exhibition in the Burns Elliot Hall [in the town centre] with your work and some of the kids'?' 'No problem.' 'We're putting you up for two nights with one of the teachers.' 'No problem . . .'

For the three weeks he was involved with Cowper, he lent us some of his work: eight framed drawings, a bronze, an unfinished plaster cast; and copies of his catalogue, which contained translations of his poems. He also left with us some Nigerian and Ghanaian textiles. I loved the drawings especially, their powerful Yoruba faces, hands, eyes; and their dynamic construction. Most of the larger ones were priced on the back at £795 plus VAT: 'My agent insists on these prices, he tells me it will be all right . . . There is a Conservative MP who has much of my work. I have explained to your teacher why it is important that he should have power . . .'

Emmanuel made it clear that we need the rich and powerful so that they can buy art. When I said that everybody needed art, not just Tory MPs, it was my second disagreement with him: the first had been when he'd commented, on the writing of poetry, that it can only be written 'when you have the feeling' (with a powerful gesture with his hands from his stomach upwards). I said that if I waited for the feeling, I'd write even fewer poems than I do, and for the first time got that British, buttoned-up sensation that Emmanuel was to leave me with many times over the following three weeks.

Still, about that time, I wrote a poem with feeling in it:

Child Asks for More Education

A 10-year-old, Rebecca Connolly,
today asked for more education
than her parents could afford.
'Please Sir', she said, shaking slightly,
'may I have some real mathematics,
not this mere arithmetic
you give me to prepare me
for the clerkly part of my future?
A long uninterrupted look
at the art section of the school library;
a session with the Nimbus LOGO program
while the boys are outside playing football;
the first mutterings of a foreign language
and a leaf through the National Song Book
(twentieth edition): "Nymphs and Shepherds"
might warm me up on days like these
that hover between sleet and hail.
And some dance would help as well
so I could mime my anger
and my parents' poverty.
My personal statement will be
a rocking from side to side,
a glance sideways, a getting up,
a knee in the Government's groin,
a getting back down, a renewed rocking . . .'
Boldly she stared out
my incomprehension

and my eventual concessions:
training in phonics and sums
and a fifteen minute go at drill
on the playground under the gaze
of Our Leader. 'Look Sir', she said,
'my brother's been put back
five years on his adenoidal op.
because of my unemployed father's
bikeless pigheadedness about BUPA
and an unwillingness to travel
two hundred miles a day
to the Nissan factory and back.
My mother is cowed to the point
where she wouldn't object to the headline
AIR IS BAD FOR YOU
as long as *The Sun* printed it.
I need to explore and make
something, however little,
and break it off from myself
and send it into the world
in the power of my spirit.
I must have education
my parents can't afford.'
I sold the story to *The Sun*
for school funds.
They led with TROUBLESOME TOT
over another piece about
LESBIAN LOONY LEFT IN RIOTS.

I held the sack open as Emmanuel cleared up the polystyrene snow after the second day. Then he looked at Jean-Marie's drawing: 'Oh, very good. That's very strong.'

I walked into the staffroom one morning to make my coffee. The room was full. Gillian said: 'I suppose even you were a whizz-kid once, Fred' and there was a silence before everyone laughed.

We had a flautist in: one of Lynda's many instrumentalists. If she leaves, I reflected, we'll be stuck for these musicians who play to the children for a bottle of wine. He was fed up with the Royal Academy of Music, and had ambitions to become a primary school teacher. While he was playing a much welcomed version of 'Walking in the Air' (from 'The Snowman'), the sounds of Emmanuel

Photograph 1: Emmanuel Jegede and Laura

Photo courtesy of Peter Smith, *The Times Educational Supplement*

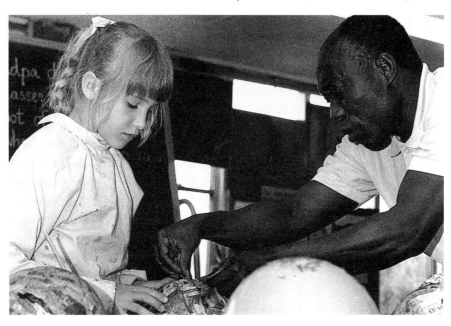

Photograph 2: Robert and Shahid work on their polystyrene cube

Photo courtesy of Terry Kenny

working with a group were clearly audible. Afterwards, one child, a tyro trumpeter, asked, 'How much puff does it take to play the flute?' The flautist demonstrated by blowing as long as he could to produce a strong and steady, then a suddenly wavering, then an eventually dying . . . note . . .

Ever since Stuart had phoned with his news, I'd been following Watford's progress. They were rough-housed out of the cup by over-vigorous Wimbledon, if *The Guardian* was to be believed — though as a South Londoner I found the notion of anything vigorous coming from Wimbledon odd. Be that as it may, Stuart's job depended on results. Will mine, soon? Who will decide what those results should be? Have I enough puff to cope with that coming, nearly-here regime?

No glory days for Watford this season, anyway. At least I have Emmanuel at Cowper, I thought to myself. And I know 'Messiah' well enough to remember 'Emmanuel' means 'God with us'.

'Justin', my note says, 'looks very ill. His hair has grown full length again, but he's pale, and only manages afternoons, and not all of those. Faye [his baby sister] is progressing well, and so is his little brother, Ben, who's been admitted to the nursery.'

Sam, who is 6, came to me in agony. He'd had lots of pain in his life so far: the break-up of his parents' marriage when he was 3, being dragged into school by me; and the frequent results of his mother's short fuse. Carol can't cope with Billy, either, Sam's younger brother. She simply can't play. When the boys get bored at home, they run round and round the immaculate coffee table in the perfectly maintained front room while Carol yells, 'Stop that! Will you two stop that!'

Biting on his playground apple had started this agony off, a creamy spotty lump outside a lower tooth. For ten minutes the agony was unrelenting. Then Sue, the secretary, calmed him down with building bricks cadged from the nursery for just this sort of purpose. Wonderfully, it turned out that Sam was a patient at the local dental clinic — and, even more wonderfully, that they would see him. Now.

But while this was going on, an adviser for special needs had turned up. Distracted by the noise from his systematic search for specific learning difficulties attached, however tenuously, to immature humans, he had found Sam. Taken him on his knee. Comforted him. This had brought the yelling on, with a renewed and chilling vigour, bringing back memories of nights broken time and time again by Daniel's unremitting crying.

As Sue forced Sam's coat on, the adviser asked me which children I would like him to see. I resisted saying, 'Here's a special need, sort this one out.' Sam was waiting quietly by now, as I put on my jacket. Eventually we got out to my elderly Cavalier. At the dentist's it emerged he'd missed his last few appointments. An abscess was diagnosed, and he was given antibiotics. I had lunch with him back at school, to make sure he had something soft, and we both showed off our stickers: 'HIP HIP HOORAY NO MORE DECAY'.

The rest of this story concerned the special needs adviser, and the telling of it in *The Times Educational Supplement* in October 1988 caused me enough trouble then, so I'm not going to put my head in the noose now. Suffice it to say, what is an abscess if not a special need? And isn't Sam's humanity devalued, not only by his mother's treatment of him, but by ours, too, the teachers', who treat him as a peg on which to hang our silly test results, our useless bits of paper, the products of our managerial systems.

I often show people round the school: prospective parents, advisers, American visitors, governors, student teachers, journalists, lecturers from local higher education institutions, new heads, probationary teachers, candidates for jobs, officers of the authority. Some of them get the grade A tour, which includes everything; others the B, which skips the problems; and yet others the C, which only includes those places on the itinerary that are of immediate concern to the visitor.

The first classroom, on the left of the front door, is Iris'. They're middle infants, and it's probably the most orderly classroom in the school. At the moment there are some immaculate drawings of tree roots, and some bright paintings that show the children have been studying Picasso's 'Model with Red Hat'. Pictures on this theme are ubiquitous in the school at the moment, but Iris' is always an artistic room — if you take the Dylan Thomasesque reprobateness out of art. Its elegance is one reason she is here, by the front door. A cynical colleague, passing through, once said to her as she was putting pictures on the display screens, 'Educating the walls again, are we, Iris?'

Children by the window are writing in large exercise books sentences under drawings they've already done in the same books. Very little of the work in here is based on the dotty world of Roger Red-Hat and Jennifer Yellow-Hat, though those two are the mainstays of the school's reading scheme. Nearly everything in here, whether 'basic skills' or not, stems from the children's experiences.

In another corner, a mother is leading a discussion about an abstract painting I can't identify, and the classroom ancillary is here too, listening to someone read. Iris would be surprised to hear this, but there is a strange, muted charisma about her teaching that makes it hard to follow: a supply teacher had some difficulties while Iris was on jury service. All is quiet, orderly, welcoming. There are no coats on the floor. One or two noisy boys will cause a spot of bother at lunchtime, with the dinner ladies — Anthony, perhaps, who fell out of his bedroom window when he was 3, and whose parents didn't get around to reporting it until persuaded to do so by the health visitor; and who can't see very well, because of his long fair hair falling over his eyes; or crop-haired Jamie, who careers into everything, bad or good, nice or nasty, with the same manic enthusiasm. But now they have their heads down: Anthony is drawing a spider plant with perfect concentration, and Jamie is fixing unifix cubes together and recording his findings.

Anthony was brought to me once with shoes that were two sizes too small for him. I lent his mother £10 to get a new pair, and she did, the following day, and she brought the money back in two instalments over the next fortnight. Anthony had been hobbling around accepting his fate, not whingeing, a true child of his times.

Iris is conscientious about computer work, and two girls are designing a tile on a program called MOSAIC, on one of the school's remaining 480Zs — one was stolen during the Christmas holidays.

The classrooms at Cowper are arranged in pairs, with links made up of toilet areas and cloakrooms. We go through one such to Gillian's classroom. This teacher sits with the children around her. They are mostly learning about phonics and number at the moment. I'm in a hurry to see Helen in Don's class, so I'm not stopping here today. I go through a shambolic area — roofed, but not protected at the sides by anything stronger than corrugated sheeting — that is used to store the Edinburgh Road drama group's flats, some woodwork tables, and a few filthy spare easels. I don't dwell on this with any of my visitors. I even pretend to some that I've never noticed it before.

The next room is Don's. The children are 10 upwards in here, and Helen's mother came to see me last Thursday, worried about her daughter's progress. I'd decided, as she made the appointment, that it would be stuff like: not enough formal maths and English to prepare her for the high school; too much fun in drama, at the painting table, and on the new Nimbus computer, which we'd bought with the insurance money for the stolen 480Z.

But the complaint was exactly the opposite: 'Helen's always loved this school, Mr Sedgwick, but now she's worried . . . she doesn't want to come to school in the mornings . . . she's doing too much arithmetic and writing . . . what about drama and painting, she loves them . . .' I'd told Don immediately. Now, I glance over at her. She's sharing a joke with a friend over a beautiful but odd painting of a four-legged ballet-dancer.

Stella's in this class. The dinner ladies worry she might be a potential anorexic, but she too is working well, looking up and smiling as I speak to her. When I get back to the office, I must ring her mother, though . . .

The Nimbus is here. Two children are drawing on the screen with the mouse, and four others are watching and advising them. 'Leave them alone', I say, and move on, through a quiet study room identical to one that all the pairs of classes share, into Barbara's room. She is hard to see at first, as she's working with Sharon, who is weak in maths. While Barbara is sitting at the child's level, she is also keeping the room observed under a broad focus. She says suddenly to Sharon, 'There you are — you CAN do it!' Sharon smiles at me anxiously, and not altogether convinced, and goes off to try on her own.

Dietrich is crying in a corner. Barbara says to me, 'I'm dealing with it — Alan called him a Nazi again.' The walls are covered with bold artwork that came from no textbook, no issue of *Art and Craft*.

Jeanette, next door, is collecting things adults say. The children offer:

Grow up girl.
Tidy your room.
Don't move your feet under the table.
Put that cat down.
Don't eat the wood shavings.
Where are your manners?
I'm going to have to send you to Mr Sedgwick.
Go down to the shops to buy me some tights.

As I leave, Jeanette commits a brilliant Spoonerism. Her 'th' sound often comes out like 'f', and when she tries to say, 'stop sucking your thumb', the effect is hilarious. The classroom is wonderful, an Aladdin's cave of displays constantly changing. Once Jeanette was late, and I took the class. When she arrived at 10.00, the children cheered. She is one of those teachers who need little technique: the person she is in her kitchen, in the park, in the pub, at a party, is the same open person she is with the children.

In Tim's room, unlucky Simon shows me his wart, which is still no better than it should be; Sara asks me if she can show her papier-mâché egg in assembly; and Danielle shows me her copy of Colin McNaughton's *There's a Lot of Wierdos in Our Neighbourhood* (Walker Books), which she'd enjoyed when I'd read it to the class.

Despite Tim's altar position in the room, he, like Barbara, is often hard to find, with his quiet voice and his unvarying reception to a distressed child: 'What's your problem, then?' Everywhere in the classroom there are mangonels that shoot screwed-up balls of paper . . . how far? . . . 1m 50cm? 1m 75cm? The children estimate, fire, measure, record.

Sue arrives in the room, and cuts this tour short. There's an insistent publisher's rep in the office, whose stuff I wouldn't give shelf room to. 'Sorry', I say. 'Can't see you now.' 'How do you choose books if you don't see reps?' 'By publishers' reputations. By reading book reviews. By having a knowledgeable staff.' He goes. His firm hasn't noticed the 1960s yet.

I sit down and write a note to Stella's mother: could she call and see me soon about Stella's progress. As the staff come up the corridor, I hear Gillian say, 'Oh well. Soon be Easter. Christmas without the carols.'

Here are some notes from a case conference on a possible child abuse:

I watched the others come in, and played the old game of guessing professions: the social workers were dressed in natural materials, and talked about 'a caring situation for the whole family' and 'a package the whole family can engage in'. The occasional moth flew up . . . The doctor said Maria, the mother of the family, 'was a silly girl who should have her tubes tied up . . . I've known her for twenty years . . .' He was the only one who argued for placement on the NAI (non-accidental injury) register. The policeman, in matching fawns and beiges, neither said anything, nor looked around the group as we assembled. Then, when he made his one contribution, there was his police dialect: clipped, yet verbose; jargony and impersonal: an understandable institutionalised attempt, I imagine, to distance himself from some of the frightening brutalities he sees . . . The health visitor looked like Dusty Springfield.

What they thought of me — smelling of school, whatever managerial smartness I'd started the day with ground away by the hubbub of art teaching, playground duty, staffroom laughter, discipline problems — goes unrecorded.

We decided, against the advice of the doctor, not to place the child on the NAI register.

Sunday evening, 9.00. I'm planning assembly and my session with the non-swimming group. The latter is easy. For the assembly, I look along Daniel's shelves for a story that will hold both the nursery children and the fourth-year juniors, but nothing catches my attention. I look through my own collection of poetry anthologies: I can't see anything there either. I put it off to the car journey to school: maybe a sermon will jump out at me when I stop at the traffic lights, or from the front page of *The Independent,* which I buy most days as a corrective to *The Guardian's* knee-jerk liberalism.

On St Patrick's Day, I felt ill when I got up, and I phoned the deputy head to say I'd be late. I had to get in, because at 12.00 we were due to interview for the summer reception teacher, and this was the only occasion when I'd been able to get chairman and adviser together.

After a hot bath, I felt better, and, when I arrived, Emmanuel was talking to Lynda's class in his loud, peremptory voice. The polystyrene sculptures were nearly ready for the plaster covering, and there was a beautiful display of drawings around the school, done by children who'd studied Emmanuel's work. He admired them with me and said, 'Western art is based on drawing, African art is based on carving . . . These sculptures will be strong, they will last twenty, maybe forty years.'

Lynda commented that, while the residency was 'great for the children', there were many administrative problems: loss of time for other things, clearing up, ordering stock. Sue also had the problem of working out how the bills are going to be paid.

But, apart from art spreading everywhere around the school, there was another enormous benefit coming from Emmanuel's presence. Black children were seeing a charismatic, successful black man who clearly deserved, and gained, the total respect of the teachers. 'This residency', he said, 'will mean that they won't see African art as quaint, or primitive, but as art in its own right, with no qualifications.'

I have no doubt that there is a residual racism at Cowper. One adult complained of Margaret that she was excitable, 'but then it is a racial characteristic'. But Matthew, also Caribbean, is slow and quiet. The racist argument would no doubt be that all blacks are high on marijuana. If you look hard enough, there'll be a stereotype to fit any situation.

Two black children are still in school one day at 4.00: 'Why is it always black children who are left behind?' Two middle-class whites are still with us the next day: 'I see Sharon's late at College again' — with the unspoken assumption that she must have a good reason. These ways of thinking are more significant than shouts of 'Nigger' on the playground.

Emmanuel tells me a story:

In Nigeria people laugh at you if you are called Jegede. A distant ancestor of mine was in court as a witness, and when the judge called him, he didn't answer. The judge said, 'Jegede, Jegede, are you sleeping?' People say that now when they hear your name is Jegede. 'Jegede, Jegede, are you sleeping?'

Later, Emmanuel said to Dawn and me, when we were asking him about the racial structure in Nigeria, 'The Yorubas are the artists, the money-makers, the politicians. They are the Jews of Nigeria.'

I arrange my room for the interviews (desk to the wall, to make more space, and to give neither the chairman nor myself anywhere to hide) and ring Edinburgh Road, to try to get our two artists together. No good — try again next week.

Mrs Hill from St Bernard's arrives to see our language teaching, and I am agreeably surprised that she won't be fobbed off by that idiotic salve of the managerially-minded teacher's conscience, the policy statement. I take her to a class, where the children are reading maths workcards and books, talking to a parent, listening, and discussing the progress of a large painting of Saint George: 'Can Mrs Hill join in your class . . .? 'But I'm not doing any language.'

The chairman is here. He reads through the application forms, as he won't be able to have copies, because the photocopier has broken down again. Neither of the two applicants I've shown around has applied, and there are only two others: a devil we know and a devil we don't. The job is to take on the large influx of children from the nursery for the last term of the school year.

Just as we're about to start, Rebecca from the Burns Elliot Museum rings. 'Would I help set up an exhibition of the artist's work, alongside work by the children, in the main hall?' 'Yes — got to go. I'll call you back.' Later Emmanuel comments, 'No problem — but I'll have to speak to my agent.'

At last the interviews get underway. The adviser is late, having been held up by a road accident. We appoint Anna, the devil we know, a jolly, open-hearted person whose manner fits in well with the school. The other candidate, when asked by the chairman, 'Would you allow parents to hear children read?' says, 'As long as it was done properly, yes.' 'Who decides what is proper?' 'Well, it has to be the professional judgment of the teacher . . .'

Shaun, whose mother objected to my putting my hand on his head, soiled himself on the day of the interviews, and neither she nor grandma was at home. The ancillary helper and the secretary washed him down while I stayed with them. I wrote to mother, and alerted the deputy to be around at 3.30 to field any complaints, because I wasn't going to be there. Nothing happened.

Damien and Mark, who pushed Simon off the wall in February, were very quiet in March. Damien's normal pallor seemed to be accentuated, and I imagined hefty fatherly pressure to prevent the boy being an embarrassment again. Mark's mother no longer brought him to school: he was catching the bus at the bottom of the hill, often as early as ten past eight, when I drove by. No reports reached me in lunchhours.

These are notes I scribbled down in the lunchhour of 21 March:

> Mr Carmello told his 5-year-old daughter's teacher, Donna, the other probationer, that Miranda had a convulsion over the weekend, the eighth of her life, and the doctor gave the family rectal valium in case it happens again. So could the teacher give her one of these suppositories if it happens in class?
>
> Donna brought him to me, and in an almost instinctively headteacherly reaction, I said I couldn't ask my teacher to do that because the other children would be in danger. I really meant, of course, as well, if not pre-eminently, I couldn't do it out of repugnance, and I wouldn't ask a teacher to do something I wouldn't do myself.
>
> I suggested that Mr C stay in school with his daughter as long as he could, and we get the LEA and the health authority to work out a plan of action: obviously it's wrong for Miranda to miss school, and the increasing use of rectal valium to curb convulsions is going to present schools with serious difficulties. He understood my position, but took M home. I phoned school health, who suggested I speak to the GP. He 'understood the teacher's reluctance'. I rang the NUT, and their advice, phoned back within the hour, was cut-and-dried:
>
> You should not have anything to do with applying rectal valium for the following reasons:
>
> 1   possible fatality (this has happened),

2   risk of AIDS and hepatitis 'B',
3   risk of allegation of sexual assualt,
4   disposal of gloves,
5   safety of other children.

In sum, as far as the union is concerned, this is a medical problem, and it is the LEA's duty to find a way of dealing with it. The NUT man went on to say that if I'd mentioned rectal valium a year ago, he'd have said, 'What?' But it is becoming an increasingly used method of treatment for fits.

'Does any teacher agree to apply it?' 'Not if they've been advised by me they don't!'

I rang the LEA, and they promised to come back as soon as possible. An adviser said, 'You realise if you won't agree to apply this medication, you're depriving this child of her rights?' Father came in next day: 'What about your nurse?' 'We don't have one.' 'We had one on the premises when I was at school, all the time.' I told him this would be a great asset.

Easter was near. When I did assembly, just after the conversation with Mr Carmello, I talked about times when we've felt deserted; then I read the story of the death of Christ from a modern version of the gospel: 'Father, why have you left me all alone?'

I taught the non-swimming top juniors, as I always do on a Monday morning, taking in some of Emmanuel's bronzes, drawings and photographs. I got the children to examine them, and to copy parts isolated by paper frames, or to write about them. Lindsey wrote:

> he's eyes are the sun with a glittery beam.
> he's pale coloured face is a sparkling stream.
> he's nose is a bridge and his face is a stream
> and he's cheek is a song on he's pale faced stream

This took about ten minutes. I went over the grammatical errors with her, and she copied out a corrected version:

> His eyes are the sun
> with a glittery beam.
> His pale-coloured face
> is a sparkling stream.
> His nose is a bridge
> and his face is a dream
> and his cheek is a song
> on his pale-faced stream.

While I was writing the notes about Miranda, Jeanette came to see me and resigned: 'I'd love to take Cowper north with me, but I can't. I've got to go, and I'm sorry . . . I know you think a year isn't very long . . .'

It had been a confused morning, but the lunchhour was far worse. I made these notes at 2.00:

12.00 Lunch with seven infants. I cut up their roast potatoes. Then I mounted the drawings I got this morning, and some of the writing (including Lindsey's), and got Danielle to help me with glue and trimmer. But while I was doing this, between 12.20 and 12.45, the phone rang four times, twice for the caretaker in his role as guardian of the authority's camping store, once with a personal call for a teacher, and 'Can I take two teachers from Podleighton CP to show round the school tomorrow?' 'Sorry, no.'

12.45 Back to the display. It was half-finished, and Danielle went out to play while I went for some coffee, leaving stapler and backing paper on a chair. But two dinner ladies intercepted me on my way to the staffroom.

'Margaret, Darren and Janey keep going behind the hedge, Mr Sedgwick, they always look as if they're up to mischief. Today Ruth (dl) caught one of them as he was dropping his trousers.'

I went to find the threesome. As I walked off, another dinner lady approached, clearly distressed, and said 'Mr Sedgwick — oh, you haven't got a minute, have you?' 'Yes.' 'We found this Cowper jumper with excrement on it and these two boys . . .' When questioned in the corridor, the two 6-year-olds pointed balefully at each other. 'He did it.' 'Wait there.' I went to find the exposer and the girls.

1.00 Darren denied it. What did you do? I swore . . . I said f and c. But that's all I did. Margaret denied doing anything that would shock the sensibilities of the dinner ladies. Janey said they were kissing. Were you kissing? Darren: Yes. Margaret: No.

1.05 But Anthony (who had the too-small shoes last term) was ill. He is subject to fits, and was now very hot. Sue and I took his shirt and trousers off, as body heat will provoke fits . . .

FREEZE.

RECAP.

Three children have probably been sexually interfering with each other to the moral outrage of a dinner lady.

Two others have defecated on a Cowper jumper (on a COWPER jumper!).

Effectively, a girl is excluded from school because I won't apply rectal valium should she take a fit . . .

Anthony (also subject to fits) is almost delirious.

NOTE TO STUDENTS OF THE BONSALL CAMPUS AT TRENT POLYTECHNIC:

— comment on the sudden rash of anal events without reference to Freud

—suggest appropriate action for the headteacher.

UNFREEZE.

1.05 I found Janice, the infant co-ordinator, and she dealt with the soiled jumper. I left the suspected interferers in the separate parts of the library, with books. I put the valium issue out of my mind (must ring the office again about that!) and Sue and I took off more of Anthony's clothes. He wept on the foldaway bed, hardly seeming to know where he was.

The family isn't on the phone, so I went to get mother, who was at a friend's house nearby. 'It's not Anthony again, is it?' I took her back with me in the car. I knew her name, Gill, from numerous case conferences, but wouldn't dream of using it for fear of sounding patronizing. Together we parcelled Anthony up in blankets and I carried him to the car ('I want my clothes!'). At home again, mother seemed unable to cope. So I said to Anthony, 'Do you want a wee?' Afterwards I carried him back to his bedroom and tucked him in. 'Has he got a teddy?' 'No.' He turned his back on the room, and his mother, and me, and cuddled his fists. My God, My God, why hast thou forsaken me? I thought, on Anthony's behalf. 'Thank you for helping me', said his mother as I left.

1.35 Back at school I told the interferers they must stay apart for the rest of the term. I said I wouldn't tell their parents this time but if it happens again . . . 'These parts of you are secret! You don't go around showing yourselves to each other!' Darren: 'I'm sorry, Sir, I promise it won't happen again.' Margaret and Janey also promised, though less fluently.

1.40 Call from the office: we're still looking into the valium issue.

1.42 I spoke to the consultant, who said: 'I agree the teacher shouldn't have to apply rectal valium with a class of children all around . . . also it's not necessary . . . it's a first aid that's very useful, but it's not vital. If she fits, and it's unlikely she will, unless she overheats, just ring 999 for an ambulance . . . pretty soon they'll be carrying rectal valium . . . Don't forget it's best if she doesn't overheat . . .'

1.50 As I went to the nursery to see Charlotte, I noticed my display in the library, half up, the stapler and the backing paper on a chair. I promised myself I would finish it after school.

Later I saw Gill:

The receptionist said the doctor wouldn't come out for Anthony, so I said that the headmaster says he's got to come and he's coming later. You have to threaten them with someone before you get any help!

A football result: Oxford 0, Watford 3. The balance after a day like that is swinging Stuart's way, even if relegation seems inevitable.

Stella's mother called about bullying. She hadn't got my letter, but she's quite happy about Stella's eating, which is fine at home. 'She's a vegetarian, but she enjoys fruit, vegetables, cheese, bread . . .' I told Sue, who told the dinner ladies.

> Thursday's the only night I can't come, it's Majorettes . . . It's my husband's orchestra night and I can't get a baby-sitter . . . No, we were not going to come, but now you've mentioned it, one of us will . . . I can't, it's my night out . . . I promise I'll try . . . I'm preparing a secret anniversary party for my mother-in-law . . . It's a ballet evening . . . I can't get a baby-sitter — 'Can't one of you come?' — Oh no, we work as a team! . . . We have guests for supper tonight . . . No, I'm not coming . . . I'll start worrying about their maths when they get to secondary school . . . I'll get along for a part of the evening, if that's all right . . .

I had telephoned about twenty parents who had not responded to an invitation to a maths evening, and this is a selection of their reasons. Jean had been planning the session for most of the term; the county's maths adviser was coming; and each teacher had set up a stall to display various activities, and was hoping to involve the parents. With the date only a week away, some of us spent time talking to parents about it at the school gate, and on the day itself, I rang around . . .

In the end thirty parents came, representing about 7 per cent of the children. I reckoned about ten of these came following our gentle bullying. As they arrived, they were greeted by a full hall: Charlotte had a table laden with equipment for early mathematical experiences; Lynda was running a stall on maths and art, and the use of the television in maths teaching; Tim had some problems to be solved; and my stall was three computers with mathematics programs set up on them.

After about half an hour I called the room to order and introduced the adviser, who was reminded yet again, and this time publicly, that he had only fifteen minutes to speak as there were sure to be questions. I presented him as a member of the committee advising the Secretary of State for Education on Mathematics in the National Curriculum.

He put the case for more use of calculators, computers, practical and problem-solving activities — 'the kind of work you see around you in this room now'. There is something reassuring about this man's appearance and manner: he looks like the perfect GP, and has much credibility with parents who might be put off by a more eccentric appearance.

Afterwards we had fifteen minutes of questions — all of them, as one of the women pointed out to me afterwards, from men. 'Why do you use metric measurement in schools when industry is using imperial?' 'Do children still learn their tables?' 'I hope you will still keep that sense of fun in learning that you have in the nursery.' One man asked, 'Aren't you de-skilling children by giving them calculators?' It was only afterwards in the pub we thought of the answer to this one: surely the invention and increased use of the washing machine had de-skilled us in the use of washboards; and what had the invention of the vacuum cleaner done to dustpan-and-brush skills?

There seemed to be amongst parents a strong feeling that what the Secretary of State had called 'pencil and paper skills' must still be imparted, whether they are relevant to tomorrow's world or not. The fact that no adult actually needs long division, or compound interest calculations, doesn't matter. So much for an education that is relevant to the needs of industry.

The parents circulated the hall, playing on computers, measuring, weighing, testing the weight a bridge could support, looking at pages of sums in the school's main scheme; or simply arguing. It was a convivial evening. There would have been more there if we'd allowed the children in to show off the equipment to their parents.

Illustration 3: Jean-Marie's drawing of Emmanuel's sculpture

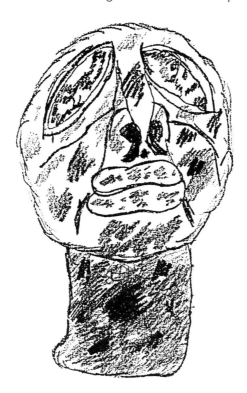

At lunchtime on the last day we drank two bottles of wine to say goodbye to Emmanuel. There was white plaster all over the library floor, and Emmanuel's palms were reddish with dye. The sculptures decorated a high shelf where the

plants used to be, and the African-coloured paintings dominated the display in the dining area. Drawings of Emmanuel's work were everywhere.

At home, Emmanuel had told Dawn and me terrible stories about the squalor of life in Lagos, and about personal tragedies. 'But', he says, 'you can't be an artist unless you have bad things happen to you.' I'd long learned to distrust this argument as much as I do its close relation: 'Artists need more love/food/drink than other people.' But Emmanuel's work as artist and teacher at Cowper has bullied me into suspending disbelief.

For the final assembly, Emmanuel agreed to say one of his poems to the whole school. 'No problem.' He recited 'Ododo Ni Mi' ('I Was a Flower') from his catalogue. The whole school, from youngest nursery child to most urbane fourth year junior, was there, in celebratory mood, to see off the term. There were twenty or so parents, too. Outside spring was at last beginning to get a grip of the weather after a damp, mild winter, and it was promising children and teachers alike a good break. As Emmanuel came to the front of the hall, he said to me, 'You read it first in English.'

I read it fast, nervously, trying to accentuate the repetition of words like 'Olabisi', 'black', 'blossoming' and 'flower'. In an English translation by Gordon Tialobi the poem begins:

I was a flower, a blossoming flower
Plucked from the bush by Olabisi,
Transplanted in a black pot by Olabisi . . .

As I finished, Emmanuel divided the school into two and said to one half, 'You go [high-pitched noise] "oo-oo". And you [the rest] go "ah-ha-SA".' Then, with both sides of his lovely rhythm section going, he said his poem. When he finished, there was a spontaneous round of applause. It was a miraculous two minutes, like the first sighting of magnolia flowers in an urban landscape, only you're expecting the magnolia.

Afterwards, as he was signing scraps of paper for the children, the staff talked about it in the staffroom: 'When are you going to sing your poems in assembly Fred?' 'Just like Graceland.' 'Did you tape it?' 'No, worse luck.' 'I wish we'd known he'd do that before, we could have got him singing in assembly ages ago.' It was as though in the last ten minutes the school and the artist had finally got to know each other.

I helped Emmanuel get his pictures, cutting files, bronze, and other sculptures to Jean's car. She was going to take him to the station, where he would catch the London train. 'How are you going to manage with all this, Emmanuel?' I imagined him between ticket hall and train, between train and taxi, with art everywhere, all over the pavement: drawings, sculptures, news cuttings about exhibitions, catalogues, textiles, ceramics. And everyone would be looking at this man and his wonderful art, all over the place. 'How are you going to manage, Emmanuel?'

'No problem. No problem.'

Chapter 3

Applications (April, May)

He advised me to keep a journal . . . fair and
undisguised. He said it would be a very good exercise
. . . I told Mr Johnson that I put down all sorts of little
incidents in it. 'Sir', said he, 'there is nothing so little for
so little a creature as man. It is by studying little things
that we attain the great knowledge of having as little
misery and as much happiness as possible.' (Boswell,
London Journal)

Why are you volunteering to take total responsibility for
every single event that takes place in a school? . . .
breakages, injuries, near riots, nervous breakdowns,
blocked drains, thefts, supporting staff in industrial
action while . . . seeking to subvert its effects, appeas-
ing parents, bullying parents, calming visitors who have
been insulted by the children/the schoolkeeper/teachers/
other visitors . . . There are those who protest that the
great thing about getting a headship is that you can
impose your . . . authority upon a school. This is
rubbish, as many a staffroom will laughingly confirm
. . . (Nick Yapp, *Bluff Your Way in Teaching*, Ravette)

All human life is there (advertising slogan for *The News of
the World*)

If I don't have the car, I either walk for the 7.45 bus from the town centre,
arriving at school at 8.00; or I go down to Donna's house, and she gets me to
school by 8.10. If I take the car, I arrive by 8.15. The first job is to pick up the
post, put the kettle on, and then look through the envelopes as the water boils.
I always hope for something interesting — that is, with my name on the
envelope, correctly spelt: an invitation to lecture somewhere, or to write an
article, or review a book. Or maybe it's proofs to check: my favourite task of all,

as it shows the thing's nearly there, but some pleasure is still to come: the last stages of a writer's foreplay. Mostly, though, it's circulars from publishers, charities soliciting fund-raising projects, letters to members of staff from their unions (or 'professional associations' as the weaselly expression has it): NUT, mostly, though there are two PAT members too.

Or maybe the local office is passing on some more of the Department of Education and Science's instructions, or the DES itself ('all replies to this communication must be prepaid') is altering the face of education in Britain.

I splash boiling water on my Kenco coffee bags, and the teachers begin to arrive; though quite often, five or six of them are at school before me. The nursery staff are always in by about 8.00. Lynda and Tim arrive next, with Gillian and Barbara; the deputy head turns up in my room at 8.20 for the day's orders, which he writes down with his fountain pen, very slowly. 'Does "Johnston" have a "t"?' He makes a small error, and borrows my Tippex to correct it. Then he posts the notice up in the staffroom so everybody can see what visitors there are today, what absences.

I overhear a conversation:

'Anyone coming today?'
'No.'
'A quiet day for a change, time to concentrate on the little herberts.'
'Lynda, have you got a tape of that programme . . .?'
'Who's on clear-up, it wasn't touched yesterday.'
[This is the rota for tidying the staffroom]
'It's Don again.'
'His mug ought to be condemned.'
'What hymns do you want to play, Gill?'
'I really couldn't care less.'
'Oh, come now Gill, that's not the attitude . . .'

The staff crowd round the notice. The spring light pours in. The phone starts next door. I gulp the last of the cooling, gritty coffee. Off we go.

The office deflated the rectal valium problem suddenly: Miranda was given a place at an observation unit for children with learning difficulties.

I had to abandon a tour of the school last term. I pick it up now. In Jean's room, she gives me a note of her impressions of the maths evening she'd very ably organized:

My first feelings when a maths evening for parents was suggested were full of enthusiasm, as I felt that parents deserved to see for themselves the sort of maths their children were being taught. Many had in the past expressed the lack of understanding of modern methods, and I thought the response would be good. After many hours of planning and discussion to try to ensure an interesting and inviting approach to the evening it was somewhat disappointing to receive such a slow and poor response to the invitation. However, after some canvassing by the head and other teachers, a few more did attend. Interest was shown in most of the activities, except (I thought rather surprisingly) for Maths in Art and TV. But perhaps because of lack of confidence not everybody actually tried them out. Afterwards a number of parents said they'd found it interesting and were glad they'd come. Hopefully this will influence attendance at any future event!

Jean told me that a teacher in another school had said our mistake was in telling the parents they'd have to do things: 'It makes them nervous!' Probably the saddest thing about the poor attendance is that it can allow teachers to take a spurious high moral ground: 'Oh well, if they're not interested in their children's education . . .' Of course parents are interested. But as one, I know that, for good or ill, so many things can get in the way of my acting on that interest: the death of a pet, City at home on the day of the Christmas Fair, writing, work, a political meeting, sheer tiredness.

In Jean's classroom there is a rich mixture on the walls. On the one hand, there is basic skills material like this:

Can you see the spelling pattern in these words?
oa
coat goat boat float etc.
and then the same for o—e, ee, ea, ou, ow, oo, ai, a—e, th, ch, —ch, sh, —sh

and, on the other hand, there are gloriously stormy, painterly sea pictures, with no corresponding evidence of basic brush-stroke skills being taught. There are also some spiky, jagged, charcoal drawings of the disco we'd held in the dome: guitarists with space-age instruments and shades, lovingly drawn amplification systems, marked 'SHARP' by Alex, the chairman's son, who is a passionate Manchester United supporter; and figures in fashionable clothes gyrating.

In this orderly, quiet room, children are set free to express themselves, and given the safety net of spelling and grammar. It is a delight to be in, though not once for a supply who'd just returned from work in Africa, and who asked me as I was about to leave her with Jean's lower juniors: 'Where's the teacher's book?' 'I'm sorry?' 'The teacher's book, with the syllabus in?' 'I'm afraid there isn't one . . .' 'Well what am I going to teach them, then?'

In the last junior room, the children are involved in three different activities. 'Normally', says Lynda, 'it's six. But I had to spend some time telling Mrs Scott what to do. Yesterday it was seven.'

'What are you doing, Shahid?'
'I've drawed a jar. I dunno what these are —'
'They're honey!'

'— and I've drawed a line across the honey jar to keep it safe. Amanda is drawing bees to go on the honey . . .'

Mrs Scott, one of our most reliable parent-helpers, and also a dinner lady, is supervising a batik session. She shows me some of the work: 'We've got a leopard skin here . . . I enjoy it, I love coming in and helping the children, and it'll set me in good stead when I'm an occupational therapist . . .' She comes in every Thursday afternoon and works on a craft idea Lynda has told her about.

It wasn't a real spring, because we hadn't had a real winter. No snow, no ice to speak of, just dampness. We thought of turning the heating off, but played safe: we hadn't got local financial control yet, and the teachers who feel the cold might as well be as comfortable as possible in what is a rather cold building. The light at the end of the day was welcome.

We require an energetic teacher at this school from September 1988.
The appointment may be made at one of three levels:
1   at entry grade. Probationary teachers should in no way be discouraged from applying.
2   at Main Professional Grade. A teacher appointed at this level will have a curricular responsibility negotiated with the head.
3   at MPG plus a C allowance. An appointment at this level will be a senior one, and the successful candidate will be expected to take a leading role in curriculum development, as well as assisting with the management of the school in terms, possibly, of home/school relations, financial management, liaison with the surrounding community, or some other area of major responsibility, as negotiated with the head.
Closing date 13 May 1988

[signed]
21/4/88

April and May are times of unrest in schools, because people are often applying for jobs, or thinking of retiring. I'd applied for a senior lecturership at a college of education in the north of England. Lynda had applied for an A allowance post for art and craft with another authority. The deputy had in two applications for headships. He asked me one morning, 'Do you know if they've shortlisted yet? . . . I haven't heard anything, I don't know whether I can write them off yet . . .?' He was very anxious until I found out from the relevant officer that shortlisting for both posts was happening the following week.

Apart from jobs, both he and I had applied for secondments — in his case, to do some work with an adviser on the early years in school, and in mine, to get some strong wind behind my becalmed PhD thesis on teaching poetry — a subject of such resolute untrendiness that no one fancied my chances. It was actually called 'Managing Poetry', in the laughable hope that this might give it a harder, more modern ring.

So the mail is interesting for at least three of us, and Lynda comes in one morning and says, 'I've got an interview.' She's been at Cowper a long time, and though she's always been popular, her colleagues hope she gets the job. I promise to do a dummy interview with her. 'I can tell you one definite thing about the head.' 'What's that?' 'He takes no notice of references.' 'What do you mean? — oh, you sod.'

I show two men around, following enquiries about our advertisement, one of them a would-be refugee from a secondary school: 'I'll get there by 12.15, I'm only down the road from your goodselves.' Your goodselves?

All the men who apply are quiet and unassertive. They do not laugh, barely smile, in fact. Have they come into primary education because it seems to be the one environment where they can control things? *Handbook of Suggestions* (HMSO, 1944), published by the Board of Education, says: 'There are some adults . . . who find in unquestioned authority over children a compensation for a feeling of inferiority towards people of their own age . . .'

The men who come to Cowper this term have a tendency towards extreme understatement and a taste in clothes that help them merge into any background likely to be experienced: all beiges, browns and bottle greens. They have no questions to ask, wouldn't dream of putting you to the trouble of answering them. Would they like tea or coffee? 'Whatever you're having — if you're having anything?' 'Actually, I usually have a large Benedictine and lime around this time of day . . .' 'I'll have the same, then . . .'

I, too, wear natural, camouflaging colours. In contrast, the women expressing an interest in this position make an immediate impression, with clothes marked *dash,* and bold reds and blues. They have plenty of questions: 'Do you have a school development plan? . . . What about RE? . . . Is your approach topic-based? . . . Would I be allowed to continue with my Advanced Diploma course? . . . How are decisions made in this school?'

After school one day, I seek out Barbara in her classroom. 'Barbara . . . how *are* decisions made at Cowper?' 'I don't know, really — that's a good question.' 'I'm worried about it — that bright lady from Essex wanted to know.' 'Let's ask Janice in the morning.'

The thump of rock music from opposite: the weather's suddenly mild, and Craig's brother can keep his bedroom window open all day if he likes. And he likes.

To the office:

> Dear Sir,
> As we have 16 women on the staff and only the one ladies' lavatory, there is frequently a serious congestion problem. Could you look into the possibility of another lavatory being supplied?

The caretaker comes back from an interview, and takes a phone call at 5.00. I can tell he hasn't got it. This is a harsh season for people in schools wanting to move. My friend George at St Xavier's goes for another headship and rings me: 'I was disappointed, not because I'm desperate to move, but because, you know, you think, I could do something for this place, and you feel rejected.' They interview for a head to replace Stuart, and don't appoint — the worst rejection of all: none of you was good enough.

Sue, the secretary, is called out for an interview at an insurance firm, and copes well with her colleagues' jokes about her smart dress. Lynda does well in her dummy interview with the chairman and myself, but we tell her, 'You didn't smile enough, and you must try to look at other members of the panel when answering questions, not just the one who's just asked you something.' Gillian has applied for a job, too. Susie, the classroom ancillary, is going, because her husband's job has moved to Hull, and so must she and the family.

> ———— has applied for a teaching post at this school, and has given your name as a referee. I would be grateful if you would let me have, in confidence, your view of her suitability for a post of this kind.
> Thank you for your help.
> Yours sincerely

A phone call at 8.45 am from Sue: 'I'm sorry, I'm going to be a bit late.' Charlotte, her daughter, is dressed as a French waitress for something at school, and won't walk. 'I'll have to drive her.' When she arrives, she tells me she didn't get the insurance job.

Sam, who had the tooth problem in March, came forestage again. His father, who is now married to someone else, appeared at the school's front door: 'I just wondered how Sam was getting on.' As he's run down his ex-wife to me before, I'm rather guarded in what I say to him: I don't want to be quoted by one of them against the other. I told him that Sam was doing well: his behavior was improving all the time. He appeared satisfied and then left. I hadn't even invited him into my room.

But five minutes later, Sam's mother, Carol, was charging over to school, pulling 4-year-old Billy along. 'Peter's been in here and I want to know why . . . If you only knew what he's doing to the children, Mr Sedgwick . . . you'll find out at the meeting on Monday . . . I can't stand much more of this, he wrecks everything I do.'

Peter is immaculate, with tidy thinning hair; clean hands, classic casual clothes; and a calm way one might either take at face value or as cynically self-serving. His ex-wife is also perfectly dressed, but thin, built like a stiletto, with a sharp face, usually smoking nervously. The prospect of the meeting at the Family Centre was a considerable anxiety.

I had to leave a staff meeting early to get there, but, not having the car, I got Barbara to drop me off. And I'd told her the wrong place. As I trudged off to the right one, about half a mile away, it began to rain, and I arrived late, wet and unheadmasterly. But the meeting hadn't started. Carol was waiting in the hall, and jerked her thumb up the stairs to show me where to go. In the room was a couple later identified as the link family — in other words, they bail Carol out when things get really bad, and take the children once a month for a weekend. Also there were the staff of the family centre, and Donal, the social worker.

Apparently, Peter had been invited. His absence led to his being gently vilified by nearly everyone: 'If he cared enough about the kids to turn up . . .' 'I can't go on with him getting at me like this . . .' It was agreed that Carol was doing 'much better lately', and that Sam was improving. I thought that if things were getting better, no doubt Carol would take the children to the dentist's next time they needed treatment . . .

When I left, the rain had stopped, so I walked across the open expanse of Municipal Park, about half a mile. When I got to the middle, it started raining again: the rain rains on the just, the unjust, and the churlish.

St George's Day, Shakespeare's birthday, the day the school opened. So up goes the scarlet and black Cowper flag, with the rampant hare on it.

A PTA committee meeting one Tuesday evening. A box of the cheapest Leibfraumilch.

At the last one (which I hadn't attended) the parents and teachers had agreed to subsidize the school journey to the Lake District, so that Margaret (who was involved in the pre-pubertal play in March that so scandalized me and a dinner lady, and who has no visible support from home) and Marcus (whose father died of throat cancer last year, and whose elderly mother is very poor) could go. I'd been delighted with these decisions.

None of the personal circumstances had been discussed. How could you talk about families in the way that would have been necessary, to convice other parents that help was needed? But several parents who hadn't been at the meeting had disagreed. 'Why should these children go if their parents can't pay?' One commented: 'Will you subsidise OUR children when the time comes?', and another pointed out that the decision was unconstitutional, as there hadn't been a quorum. The deputy head, visibly under pressure, declared the meeting invalid, and called another one, tonight's. Agenda:

> Apologies
> Minutes of previous meeting
> Matters arising
> Report on meeting of 14 March: No quorum
> Discussion of constitution
> Treasurer's report
> Summer Fair progress report
> Any other business
> Date of next meeting (Summer Funday).

This bland list disguised the tension.

The deputy talked at length about the reason for tonight's meeting. He was characteristically meticulous, and his attention to detail meant that, after ten minutes, no one else had spoken:

> It seems that the decision — which I entirely stand by, I might say (and I suspect, with good reason, that Fred does too) — I think it was a good decision, and the fact that it doesn't comply with the constitution as it stands is another matter, an equally important matter . . . in any case, I've called this meeting because I, we, don't want anything to be under cover, to be done without the full consent of this committee. I think it right that this matter be discussed fully now . . .

One parent was incensed, and Heseltined out. The others voted (with Janice's support) that the decision was wrong. I said, bitter as bile, 'OK, do what you like, we'll find a way to finance the journey for those kids somehow.'

Next morning a cheque was to come from one of the parents who thought the matter had been badly handled by the deputy and me: '£30 for Margaret's journey to the Lakes'.

The rest of the meeting was routine and compensatingly polite: all about the impending funday (fair). We noted that I'm to write to local schools about a five-a-side football competition.

> Behind my face
> and inside my head
> the blood rushes
> like people running
> to catch a train
> in a far-off station
> which is beyond the stars.

Through my brain
rattles the days
of the past
and the bad and good.

Over my mind
passes round the work
that has to be done.

Along the silent path
that is secret
there will be red roses
that are prisoned
in my brain.

Emma Carson (10) wrote this one Monday morning when she couldn't swim because of a cold. The stimulus was no more than the idea of the prepositional phrase, and how it might unlock ideas. I'd got it from Pie Corbett and Brian Moses' book, *Catapults and Kingfishers* (Oxford University Press).

I'd sent *The Times Educational Supplement* an article about Emmanuel, and the features editor rang: she liked the piece, but the photographs Tim had taken were not good enough 'in newspaper terms'. She would send a photographer to the school, and pay Emmanuel to come back and work with the children for an hour, to get photographs that would look good alongside the article.

On the day chosen, Lynda's class were out on a walk, so we used Tim's class as understudies. Lynda and I set up the room during hymn practice and coffee break, and by 10.55, five minutes before Emmanuel and the photographer, Peter Smith, were due to arrive, the children were working on a passable simulation of nearly everything Emmanuel had done with Lynda's class. I began my neurotic wandering between the classroom and the carpark, willing the next car to be either Emmanuel's taxi or Peter's car.

Charlotte appeared in the classroom at 11.25 with Peter. 'Would you like some coffee?' 'Yes please, milk and one sugar.' 'I'm afraid Emmanuel isn't here yet.' 'Don't worry, I'll get the feel of the place.' We put his mug on the teacher's desk, and within a minute he was doing his complicated photographer thing: lining up shots and angles, genuflecting before groups of children who immediately learned to ignore him.

11.35, and there was still no sign of Emmanuel, so I rang the station. 'The next train in is due any minute now . . . 11.37.' Sally, the nursery nurse, drove down, and five minutes later re-appeared with Emmanuel in the front passenger seat and, behind, his wife and their baby daughter. As only a quarter of the time for the session we'd planned was left, I whizzed him into the classroom, and he was working with the children in seconds, exchanging greetings with

Lynda simultaneously. Peter, on his second cup of milky, sweet coffee, knelt and clicked, climbed on chairs, put a huge silver circle behind groups of children, and seemed satisfied.

Later Barbara found Emmanuel's wife feeding the baby in the ladies' lavatory, and brought her into the vacant deputy's office. Later still she had a school salad with her husband and Peter, while I ran a disco in the dome with five of the staff.

Sally agreed to take Emmanuel and his family back to the station: 'I'll send you a copy of the article, of course I will . . . Do come again, won't you? . . .' 'Oh yes, we love ———shire . . .' I collected my salad, made some tea, closed the door and put my feet on the desk.

Sally put her head in: 'I've got a flat tyre.' We transferred the travellers to Charlotte's Renault, and this time they made it.

Letter to eight local primaries:

> Dear ———,
> We are hoping to organise, on our PTA funday on Sunday afternoon 20 May, a five-a-side football tournament. Would you like to bring a team along? We can arrange refereeing etc., though any help would be appreciated.
> Could you let Don Snaid or me know if you can come.
> Yours sincerely

Letter from Grigson CP:

> Dear Fred,
> Thank you for your letter about the five-a-side football on your funday. But I'm afraid we draw the line at school activities on Sundays!
> Yours sincerely

Letter from a college in the north of England:

> Dear Mr Sedgwick,
> We have received a large number of excellent applications for the post for which you have applied, and we have taken up references on ten of the candidates. This letter is to let you know that you are on this list.
> The short list will be drawn up as soon as possible, and we will let you know immediately, possibly by telephone as well as a letter, if you are on that short list.

In view of the tight timescale, we thought it would be useful for you to have this information.

Yours sincerely

Letter from a parent:

Dear Mr Sedgwick,

George will be terminating his cello lessons forthwith as Mr Holbrook insists he practices at home. We feel that Mr Holbrook does not appreciate the not inconsiderable burden this places on a family. Perhaps George might take up another instrument at the beginning of the next academic year.

Yours sincerely

Letter from the local education authority:

Dear Mr Sedgwick,

Thank you for your letter concerning your PhD studies . . . Whilst being very interested in the topic of your study (Managing Poetry) we are unfortunately unable to offer you release or secondment from your duties to continue your studies on that basis . . . We would, of course, be happy to continue meeting your University fees if they have been met by the LEA in the past . . .

Yours sincerely

Two teachers and a parent run a bookshop every week during the Wednesday lunchhour. As I write these notes, there are thirty children sitting in the library, reading and talking about books: funny books (*Don't Forget the Bacon*, by Pat Hutchins, for example), tiny books with few words, factual books. Two girls are lying stretched out on large scatter cushions, reading poems to each other, from Kit Wright's *Hot Dog*. There is a dinner lady helping an infant to choose, and two fourth-years are taking the money and handing out stamps and books.

I give these two £1.89 for a book for Daniel — 1p short, but they don't notice. Abigail kisses Charmaine on the cheek, and Charmaine is cross about it. Shahid stops on his way out to play to point out to friends the fish in Tim's tank. Mark comes by, and looks too. There's been no trouble since that fracas in February, but I don't believe that hefty disciplinarian styles have a long-term effect on bullying. It's made life easier, though, for the time being: for me, for Simon, and arguably for Mark himself.

The adults are trying to eat their school lunch as they run the show. This is a valuable time for the children, but how can teachers teach at their best when they haven't had any break at all in the middle of the day? On Wednesdays it's bookshop, on another day it'll be a liaison meeting with Edinburgh Road, or a curriculum planning meeting at Cowper, or a discussion about a child. Barbara and her colleagues are on the go, as my mother would put it, all the time.

'I'm buying this one for my little brother.' Barbara puts down her fork, takes the stamps, and sends the child happily out to play. Simon appears beside me: 'My wart's gone, Mr Sedgwick.'

As the bookshop closes, the drop-in opens at the infant end of the school. There are only two parents there at 1.15: six foot tall, pregnant Jen, and tiny, noisy, cheerful-in-spite-of-everything Chris, whose husband, she says — and I believe her — sells the kids' toys at car boot sales for beer money. Now the two women sit among the drop-in's toys with their toddlers, discussing whether, following legislation just gone through the Commons, they're entitled to free meals anymore. They almost certainly aren't: as the law bites, our dinner numbers, which depend largely on free meals, have fallen from 130 to 80. The school meals people worry, understandably, about their jobs. We all (except the Government) worry about the children's diet.

Two more parents turn up. Estelle, who paints watercolours, and who has just illustrated a book, comes in out of the bright cold with her son, Edward, and then Mrs Carroway arrives. Twenty minutes later, after I've gone and come back, there are more: Vera, who holds the whole thing together, and Mrs Snelling, who discusses City's fortunes with me, are two of them. Her 14-year-old son is said to be interesting Stuart Murdoch at Watford. Another mother is reading a story to a group of six infants from Donna's class next door.

The other women are chatting in groups, and six juniors are drawing a stuffed kestrel just outside the open door. I am teaching them, but by placing myself here I can do most parts of two things at once. In fact, it is useful that the parents in the drop-in can offer the children extra encouragement. Estelle can offer technical advice.

Fifteen applications have arrived for the C allowance post, and about forty for the post at Main Professional Grade (MPG), the basic scale. Many of the latter are from students in their final year of BEd degree or Post Graduate Certificate of Education (PGCE) courses.

One reason for early dismissal is often the expression 'committed Christian'. This is emphatically not because of a bias against Christianity, but because 'committed' is a mean-hearted shorthand that says: other teachers may call themselves Christians, but with me you've got the real thing. It is a code, in fact, for 'evangelical' or (these days) 'charismatic'. Such applicants are telling me more than I want to know at this stage. Certainly I am interested in their religion, their politics, whether they are vegetarian, vegan or unilateralists. But, as Augustine said, not yet.

Other candidates are applying from posts in private education. I don't hold this against them anymore, because they are often there only because they couldn't get a job in the state sector at the right time. One such has applied, and I've written to her headteacher. Two weeks to the day after my letter, he rings. Sue puts him through:

> Fred Sedgwick here.
>
> Fred Tyson here! [mutual congratulation of Freds] Now about Mrs Lambert. She's a super girl. Does maths and geography with my 10-year-olds, can't speak for her with younger ones, but she's a credit to this place . . .
>
> Can I have something in writing? My authority won't let me appoint without a written reference.
>
> OK, but she's fine. I should think having a BSc on the staff would be a feather in a state school's cap, especially a primary school . . .

One candidate says she is interested in 'synchronized swimming and playing the flute'.

While the file is thickening encouragingly with green forms (Personal interests? it asks, and I read in my sleep: Reading, travel, swimming and listening to music), the deputy head is getting desperate until, one Friday evening, he rings to tell me he has an interview at a two-teacher school a mile outside the City boundary. He's been after a headship for four years, and has had six interviews. I wish him well, sincerely.

Every day I show a couple of candidates around. Then a letter comes from the north of England college:

> Dear Mr Sedgwick,
> Further to my letter of ———— and your application for the post of Lecturer in Primary Education, the Warden has asked me to write to you to invite you to come to the College for an interview on ————.
> I enclose a map of the College site; you will find a space for parking inside entrance 2. You will be met at the Lodge. I enclose . . .
>
> After coffee, formal interviews will take place before and after lunch. As part of the procedure, you will be asked to take a short discussion (about half an hour) with a group of students from the final year. I attach a summary of the Kingman Report on which you should base the discussion.
>
> Please confirm that you can attend.
> Yours sincerely

It was in anticipation of this interview that I went to the termly meeting of primary heads. Agenda: privatization of groundstaff, cleaning and school meals;

and Local Financial Management (now re-named Local Management of schools). An administrator has come to tell us the bad news about the privatization plans. I feel sorry for him, because he probably doesn't approve of them. But as he says, 'why shoot the messenger?' He is a steely, handsome man in the obligatory smart suit. I envy him his fitness — he probably jogs and doesn't drink, I muse sourly — but not his role. I also envy him his grasp of detail, his conscientiousness about trivia, which a good administrator (and he is that) must have.

His delivery enacts an antonym for 'showy' or 'vulgar'. He must assume that what he's saying is so interesting that we're all agog. But it's a fallacy that bad news always rivets our attention, and, in any case, we've gleaned most of this stuff from circulars. He is like that character in Powell's *Dance to the Music of Time* who has been so long in the viscera of administration that circular codes, interim agreements, salary structures and green papers have more reality for him than flesh and blood, or love and pain, or a Stilton Ploughman's and a pint.

Outside a blackbird bemoans the loss of a tree: a loss we'd noted last October. The sky is a 'blue true dream' and I wish I were walking out there now. There is a bird homelessness problem, and Charlotte bets the Government is doing nothing about it . . . The administrator goes on, like a method actor asked to suggest total indifference to some fearsome tragedy: 'Hopefully it will be helpful . . . You'll be getting much more paperwork . . . We're still working on the fine detail . . . We have to implement these instructions by 1991 . . .'

Someone asks about lettings, and he answers about caretakers. One head, Ms ex-ILEA, asks why the authority has not arranged consultation with professional associations over these proposals, and Mr Dangerous Radical comments roughly from the floor: 'What good's consultation? It's the Government who's responsible for this mayhem, not the LEA, and when you ask for consultation with them, all you get is a bloody nose . . . How many of us have told our parents about the effects of this Government's policies?' DR looks round challengingly and sits down in an icy atmosphere. He assumes, you can tell, that most of his colleagues were more than happy to vote this Government in.

Ms ex-ILEA and Mr Dangerous Radical are only two of the characters present. Here is Mr My-school, who uses that expression eight times in three minutes. *His* school? And Mrs Subservient. When the administrator says we must 'tolerate administrative complexity in the early stages', she writes 'Tolerate admin. complex. in early stages' in her notebook.

Another character here is Mr Old-Stager, who's seen it all before. He's talking about the new A,B, and C allowances, and he remembers the divisive effect of posts of special responsibility in 1959, was it? We got over it then, we'll get over it this time. His look of good-natured scepticism belies the savagery with which he'll attack the LEA in his Volvo on the way back to school.

And there are the bad lads . . . though Stuart is gone: in the Second

Division, by now, which is the richer for his presence, as we are the poorer. So the bad lads look glum, and wonder what other work they could do. One thinks of turning his sports journalism into a full-time job, another talks darkly of taxi-driving, another of selling more articles about . . . what was that? Seriously? Vegetarian cookery?

From *The Guardian,* 31 May 1988, a middle school head talking:

> . . . if I had wanted to run a business I would have done it at 16 and joined my dad who had a very successful ironmongery business in the Midlands. I chose to come into education and now these cowboys in government are changing the system. I'm not surprised if people don't want to do the job.

Back at school there's a note from Stuart. At the top is 'WATFORD' in one-inch-high scarlet letters, and the logo at the bottom is a yellow goalkeeper letting a high one in. Very appropriate.

> Dear Fred,
> How the hell are you? Sorry I haven't been in touch, life has been very hectic . . .

He goes on to ask about the heads who were appointed about the same time as the two of us. While I'm reading, two boys are brought in. Fighting. 'Who started it?' 'He did.' 'He did.' A thousand years in headship will not teach me to deal with this one.

> Jason: He couldn't take losing, and he punched me in the back. My bad back an' all —
> Ian: He chased after me and told me to f off. He took the ball and hit me so I hit him back. I've got witnesses —

The barrack room lawyer never learns. Afterwards, he gazes upwards like an El Greco saint. Then both boys have lunch in my room, at different times.

Later in the same day, Jan was brought to me holding his stomach and looking pale in the face. Graham and Steven had stepped on (Graham) and sat on (Steven) Jan during the rumbustious fighting that characterizes the play of these boys. I made Graham and Steven tell their mothers on the telephone what had happened, and rang Jan's mother myself. 'He's quite capable of swinging the lead', she said. Jan was basking in his misfortune and tomorrow the GP would diagnose internal bruising.

Next, I rang my friend Geoff to talk about a course we were working together on next term and this book, when Sue came to the door. 'Crisis', she said. 'Crisis, Geoff, I've got to go.' Two parents, mother and father of 6-year-old Conor, were rumoured to be bashing each other in the infant general purpose area. But when Sue and I got there, there was only the dust rising gently, and a few mutterings. Conor and his parents had gone. No one told us anything about it.

The Fight

There's a fight on the playground today —
    Two big boys from Mr Magee's
Are knocking the daylights out of each other
    Under the trees.

The girls are silent and staring
    And Clare whispers 'Stop it Paul'
As the fighting gets wilder, and feet jab out
    And fingers maul.

I watch, and I'm glad it's not Joe
    And me in that horrible space —
Not my stomach winded, not my nose bleeding,
    Not my burning face.

The sky is bright. Two planes fly
    Out from the base, while one
Boy holds the other down with his knee
    And breathes, 'You done?'

There's a fight on the playground today —
    Paul Topple from Mr Magee's
Is crushing the daylights out of John Randall
    Under the trees.

A Friday evening. I was just about to open the Valpol when the deputy rang: 'I got it!' Congratulations and relief all round. And a flow diagram to work out where we go from here, because the appointment came too late to allow us to appoint a deputy for next term.

A Monday morning. Sue rings: 'Sorry, I'll be late, but the hamster's dying and I must get it put down.'

A candidate I'm showing round mentions a teacher I know as a contributor to *The Times Educational Supplement:* 'He's my mentor.' Then, later: 'I'm a progressive. But my husband, he runs a small electrical firm, and he says young people haven't got the basic skills . . . I still think children need the basic skills . . .'

It rained all day during the funday, but it was the most successful we'd ever had, raising over £800. The part I was most involved in, the five-a-side football, had to be put into the sports dome, and it was, of course, very cramped, with eight teams of boys, men who unironically termed themselves 'managers', and supporters all crammed round the edges.

Elsewhere, cakes went like hot ones, the tea-stall steamed through the afternoon, second-hand books were reduced and reduced until you could have got an armful of romantic fiction or cowboy stories for 2p, and toys and white elephants disappeared. Sue sat in the staffroom, smoking John Players, putting coins in plastic counting trays and adding up columns of figures.

How this genial shambles attracts anyone, or makes money, is beyond me, but it does both. In the bar tent, outside, six people sat through the afternoon drinking and listening to the rain hit the canvas. David the caretaker had got in four St Edmund Ales for me, and I drank them.

Lynda went off to Shropshire for two days for her interview:

> I didn't get it . . . I don't know if I wanted it, really . . . the panel was the head, the deputy and two other teachers — no, no governors, no advisers, no officers, no inspectors — I was the only one being interviewed, the others were done earlier in the week . . . You'd have been appalled at the art and display, Fred! They need me, but I don't need them! . . . I wasn't even given a cup of tea or an expenses form! . . .

But Lynda did need them, because she was desperate to move to that part of England. She left her application in for a main scale post for art at the same school. Once again the head interviewed in stages, and didn't need to see Lynda again. He told her he'd let her know when he'd interviewed two other candidates. Lynda felt hopeful. Then he rang me: 'Stan Matthews here [he then named the school]. Could I leave a message for Mrs Noah? . . . I'm afraid we're not offering her the position . . .'

> Oh bugger him! [said Lynda] . . . I don't care! . . . When I talked about this school, how big it was, how much space all the rooms have, I told him about you. 'Our head goes on trips, teaches with you sometimes . . .' He said, 'Sounds like management by walkabout!'

Jeanette found out that she wasn't getting an interview for her job in the north. The deputy brought in Chianti and Leibfraumilch to celebrate his headship. Four years ago, he'd said how a small school wouldn't suit him. But now he's as happy as possible with this forty-child one.

A reference comes, for one of my candidates: five pages long. I reply:

> Dear ————,
> Re: your notes on Mrs Barnard. Please expand.
> Yours sincerely

but am dissuaded from sending it.

> The Education Catering Service has a healthy eating policy in which
> the successful candidate will be expected to take an active part. (From
> an advertisement for the job of cook in a nearby school)

Tomorrow I'm going for my first interview in five years, so I turn up at a lecture
on a heads' course I'd thought I'd avoid: I'm promised it will bring me up to
date on the TGAT report (on assessment and testing).

It seems we should be grateful for the report. It avoids the worst excesses
of the input-output model the DES favours: 'TGAT is flexible in its ten stages,
vastly better than 11+ type pencil and paper testing.' But the language (I argue
over-heatedly) is anti-human. Objectives (or targets, as we call them these days)
miss the messiness, the richness of education. They deal well with the more
functional reaches of learning, largely concerned with training rather than
education: low-level skills rather than concepts. But they cannot handle the
deep structures of a subject, which are profoundly related to the serious
questions we ask children to consider in the humanities, the arts and the
sciences.

And targets are not interested in *now*. They focus entirely on what Norman
Nicholson calls 'rising soon'. They concentrate on a narrow path, ignoring the
flowers that grow away from the path which are, as Joan Sallis said recently at a
lecture up the road at Glenbrook, the best ones. I suspect that the Government
does not want us to see the flowers, for fear we should be distracted from the
business in hand, the making of more money.

I'd thought Lawrence Stenhouse had won this battle in 1975 in Chapter 6
of *An Introduction to Curriculum Research and Development*. But, of course, we
don't have a Government likely to be won over by intellectual clarity.

I say something like all this, and Reg, a colleague, asks over his coffee cup:
'Why do you say these things, Fred? The horse has bolted, we've got to get on
with living as things are . . . It's eloquent, what you say, and it's what a lot of
us are thinking, but why bother? Now?'

Later I show him a sentence from a review of the report, as an example of
why I still bother: '"Schools must evaluate their assessment procedures." Then
surely, Reg, they must assess the evaluation of their assessment procedures.
And they they must evaluate the assessment of the evaluation of the assessment
procedures . . .' The sentence goes nowhere . . . 'Oh dear', he replies. 'Life
must be very painful for you, Fred.'

I should have said at this point (Charlotte rightly tells me later), 'Life will
be painful for *you* in a minute, mate.' But all I can do is burst out laughing, and
mince off with a limp wrist. 'Ooh yes, Reg. I'm *that* sensitive!'

I put on my dark grey interview suit, a new light grey shirt, and the black shoes we'd chosen for our wedding, eight years ago. I chose a pink and grey tie, and folded it carefully in my left-hand jacket pocket. I'd not been in a college of education since I'd qualified in 1968.

Stonely turned out to be like St Luke's (Exeter) in its casual countryside beauty and its genteel atmosphere, except that while St Luke's had been designed (as its prospectus had told us in 1965) for 'the education of Christian gentlemen', Stonely concentrates now on the training of the daughters (mostly) of gentlefolk for positions in both private and state education. These are students making their confident way in other tracts of Mrs Thatcher's Britain, as well as its schools. One young woman said too me, 'I'm sorry, I'm going into an advertising agency.'

The photographs in the prospectus turned out to be true reflections of the place: healthy young women made up for rag day or graduation; or posing in enormous study bedrooms, reading Piaget, or whatever was closest to hand when the photographer turned up — a pair of whitened tennis shoes neatly in shot alongside a racket. Some pictures were humanless: willow trees, for example, falling across a northern river; or magnolia and cow parsley wild behind the old part of the building. Or the modernistic library.

All the lecturers in this prospectus (I later discovered this was common in higher education) were listed with a peculiar fullness: 'L. Mary Robinson BA (Sheffield) MEd (Cantab) CertEd (Somewhere Else) Advanced CertEd (Somewhere Else Again)'.

They met me at the Lodge. I was taken for coffee in the wood-panelled, elegant Senior Common Room. The coffee was fresh and strong, and much needed after my preparations the night before. The Warden briefed us, and another lecturer told us about the interviews and the session with students.

The interviews were a disturbing mixture of the practical ('How do you make effective classroom teachers?') and the theoretical ('What linguistic theorists are you familiar with?'). A lecturer observed the session with the students. I avoided the sherry by gulping orange juice, and skirted social problems at lunch (I assume) by not dropping any of my breaded plaice into my lap, or grinning incredulously at any opinions expressed. I spent the rest of the time talking with my rivals, all women heads, and hoping I'd get the job. I'd love to work here, I thought. I love that library.

The Warden said he'd telephone us later. At home, I went over the day with Dawn. Daniel began to develop his migraine symptoms, and, as he vomited for the first time, there was a knock on the front door: an elderly neighbour, to discuss a problem common in our area, subsidence. The phone rang: the Warden. 'We had an embarrassment of riches . . . you interviewed very well . . . but I think you'll've gathered that the news isn't what I think you were hoping for . . . If we advertise another post, do look in our direction . . . I'm sorry it isn't better news . . .'

A pale Daniel came down the stairs. My neighbour was still there on the doorstep. Apparently, his house has been sinking for ten years.

Phone call:

> Cowper School. Can I help you?
> Please can I have a form for the post advertised in the circular? I'm at Glenhavon at the present.
> Certainly. Shall I send it there?
> I'd sooner you sent it to my home, if you don't mind. (This said as though I'd made an improper suggestion.)

Sue was upset: 'Justin was ill, so I walked with him from his classroom to the library and rang his Auntie Margie, as mum isn't well. On the way he wobbled a bit, and I said, "Justin, are you all right?" and he said, "Do you really expect me to be?"' His left arm hangs, and his left leg is not as efficient as it was.

The next day, I talked to Justin while his aunt was dropping Ben off. 'Can I read you a story, Justin?' 'Yes.' I picked a book at random, out of the nursery book tray, all about a Sikh boy getting dressed, and read it. He looked intently at every page, and read some of the words for me. Then I took him off to his infant class, and yes, he was wobbly.

Some infants did a tour of the school with Jackie, a part-time teacher. She'd read them a translation of Miroslav Holub's poem, 'Go and Open the Door', and when she got back to the library, she wrote down their words:

> Open the door.
> There are some children
> climbing, swinging, up ropes,
> moving in different ways
> through, over and round,
> hanging upside down.
>
> Open the door.
> It's locked.
> Could be a monster,
> could be a ghost,
> a unicorn person,
> a wonderland,
> a marshmallow man.
>
> Open the door.
> A Christmas cupboard,
> decorations, lights,
> red, green, sparkly,
> all different colours,
> glittery lights.

66

Two fairies are looking for teeth.
When the light's off
it's dark and scary.

Open the door.
There's flowers behind it,
trees, daisies, buttercups, grass.
It's lovely and sunny.
The sky is blue
with fluffy clouds.

Open the door.
A classroom covered with paintings,
masks on the wall
painted all different colours.
A toy looks like the sun.
There's a birthday boy, he's 9,
a puppet all tangled up.
It's Mr Big Ears,
spring on his head,
no hair,
red cheeks,
chubby nose,
smily face, popping out eyeballs.
A classroom covered with children
writing, drawing, laughing, smiling,
talking, lots of friends together.

Open the door.
Messy. Junk.
Paints, red folders, paper,
jars, lots of flower pots, lego,
potatoes, dirt,
clipboards, chess horse, boxes, crayons,
all different stuff.
Gold paper.
More like a junkyard,
more like a pigsty.

Part of my school tour:

Next to the nursery is probationer Donna's reception class, where the children offer one of the warmest welcomes in the school. And this welcome has no hint of a vested interest . . .

Certainly they greet you lavishly in Tim's room, for example, but there children say, 'Can I show my model' (of a marble-carrying slide that changes direction three times) 'in assembly please?' Or, 'Here's my painting of a archeopteryx . . .'

And you're welcome everywhere else. With Jean's 8-year-olds: 'I've got that book of poems you read to us!' Or in Janice's, where a voiceless boy waves a bit of paper: 'It's the first sentence he's ever written, if you've a moment . . .'

But you feel less welcome in the top juniors, where sophistication has made inroads into childlikeness. Where to put away childish things seems aspirant towards, not so much grace, as danger, and decadence. Here it is better to be cool and wicked, than to please the headmaster, who comes round, looking over your shoulder, to see if your calculations are right, or your descriptions interesting. To see whether you are using as many different kinds of brush-stroke as you can think of. To see, in other words, whether you are behaving like a potential secondary school student.

With the top juniors there is evidence of a sub-culture: conversations about television, advertising, pop music, magazines. And teacher-life is problematical and complex, welcomes less ready, where the raucous world of commercial reality is arriving. Do we care if he likes our stuff? We do not!

. . . But in Donna's, they shout, 'Hello' across the room, whether or not (to Donna's credit) it's Donna, or a supply teacher.

Two fourth year juniors are here, helping the young infants with the LOGO program; in particular, getting the turtle, a machine they control with instructions fed into the computer, to move round a large piece of white paper. It leaves a trail drawn by a felt tip pen fixed into it. 'FORWARD 30 LEFT 90 FORWARD 30 LEFT 90', etc. The children are confronting geometry in a systematic way for the first time, and the experience is a vivid one, but there is a problem in the large technical failure rate: the pen isn't properly loaded, or a connection has failed, or the battery needs re-charging, or the wires foul the thing's slow progress. I note again that the shape on the monitor which is supposed to be a map of the shape on the white paper isn't a square at all, because of the convex design of the screen.

In another part of the room, seven 5-year-olds are covering food containers with paper. I catch a glimpse of Donna's lesson notes:

> The children will cover variously shaped boxes with paper. This is an early stage in the exploration of the concept of area: they have to work out how much each box will need, as they try to leave no part of each box uncovered . . . Another group will work with triangles, covering flat areas, trying to make sure that there are no gaps left.

As I go over to a group examining an abstract print the school has just bought (with the help of a subsidy from the Art Adviser), I reflect that teachers are probably the only people who use the word 'tesselation'.

A parent is with the art group, pointing out to them the various shapes in the print:

'What's this shape?'

'It's a, it's a circle —'

'Half a circle!'

'That's right, Anna-Marie. Half a circle, a semi-circle. And what's this one, here?'

'That's got a circle at the end —'

'But it's long — '

'It's got straight lines too.'

'We call this one a cylinder.'

On the last Monday of the half, we interviewed — chairman, adviser and I — for the vacancy caused by Jeanette's resignation. It had only been a year since I'd put my head round the staffroom door after an interviewing bout like this and said, 'Would you like to come back in for a moment?' — observing the quaint tradition that we might be calling her back for amplification to some answer, or even to ask another set of questions.

But as you go through that formula, of course, you daren't look at the other candidates, because their expressions are bound to be saying, 'Oh well, that's that then.' I heard a rival say, in a surprised tone, as I was called back under these circumstances at Cowper in 1984, 'Oh, he's got it then', but I was too busy throwing an imaginary cap in the air, and miming a quick chorus of 'Oo-oo-oo, what a little moonlight can do-oo-oo', to care.

We were to see twelve candidates on this occasion, four for the C allowance, a senior post just under the deputy headship, and eight for the basic job on the main grade. There were that many because, when we'd shortlisted, there had been a strong possibility of at least one other vacancy — Lynda was applying with considerable consistency and vigour — and usually someone withdraws. But Lynda had still not got a new job, and no one had withdrawn.

In the end we appointed a quiet young woman, Helena, to the MPG. She promised to take over the library and resources from Barbara, and seemed surprised and pleased when we offered her the job. Barbara, one of the internal candidates, was given the C allowance, and told she would be responsible for helping the school to come to terms with the impending National Curriculum. This was a popular appointment with the staff — except, of course, for the other internal candidate.

As the half ended, the only teacher (apart from Barbara) with any reason to celebrate success in the applications stakes — the deputy — was away ill. We finished with a large number of supply teachers.

As I walked round on the last day, Lynda said, 'Did you ever do anything about Mark's smells?' 'No, I forgot.' 'It's bad, the other children are taking the micky . . .' So I phoned his grandfather at British Rail:

'Mr Leach, two things. The first is, Mark's behaviour. It's been much better lately, and it's only fair that, if I complain when it's bad, I should give him his due the rest of the time . . . The second thing is, to be frank, Mr Leach, he smells rather badly . . .'

'I know. And I know what it is, I had it when I was a lad. It's nerves, Mr Sedgwick . . .'

'But could you get him seen at the doctor's? He's getting some stick from the other children and I'm sure you'll appreciate how unpleasant this must be for him . . .'

'I'll do that . . . and thank you for telling me.'

I was preparing assembly when Charlotte knocked and came in. 'Have you got a moment? Two children have just turned up in the nursery, one's deaf, one's Marie-Claire's little brother . . . they shouldn't be here . . .' Charlotte had brought them along: a thin, vague-faced 8-year-old girl with a prominent hearing aid on each side of her head, and a cheerful little boy who was clearly enjoying the adventure. I asked Charlotte to find 7-year-old Marie-Claire and send her up.

'That's Kerry, there's no use talking to her, she's deaf, she doesn't understand anything, not even a little bit . . . and that's Chrissie, my little brother.'

I got out the building apparatus kept for this purpose and rang Marie-Claire's mother:

'Oh God . . . they've got away from the child-minder again . . . I'll phone her and ring you back.'

Two minutes later:

'The child-minder's expecting the gasman, but Kerry's mother's coming.'

In fact a man turned up. 'Are you Kerry's father?' 'No, I'm the boyfriend . . . You [to Kerry, very clearly enunciated] are in trouble. [To me] I've been all over the estate looking for them. Come on you lot.'

I didn't have the car at school, so I enjoyed myself walking home. Through St George's Close, all close-packed housing and graffiti; down St George's Drive, between the high school and the special school on the one side, and the Catholic public school on the other; across Municipal Park, where Daniel and I play and watch football on Sunday mornings, much as my brother and I used to thirty years ago in London; across the railway, and then across the river, to the part beyond the reach of Kerry's mother's boyfriend, and Mr Leach, and Carol and Sam and Billy, that I live in.

Chapter 4

Wish You Were Here (June, July)

We were a noisy crew; the sun in heaven
Beheld no vales more beautiful than ours;
Nor saw a band in happiness and joy
Richer . . .

(Wordsworth, *The Prelude*)

What dreadful hot weather we have! It keeps me in a
continual state of inelegance. (Jane Austen, *Letters*, 18
September 1796)

The weather is hot. The pollarded birch is a rich apple green. At the beginning
of school, the children spread over the field, and the first richnesses of summer
float unused by . . . At least, that's how it seems to the teachers as they make
coffee on arrival. The phone rings:
8.15 am Mrs Ferenz from Harlech CP: Could she interview Mr Sedgwick about
his views on primary management? She's read a piece of his in *The Times
Educational Supplement* that interested her . . . 'Master under God' wasn't it?
. . . We arrange a date. 'You'll recognise me — I'll be the person with the
notebook!'

8.20 Alec Jennings (infant) won't be in: sickness and diarrhoea. 'Stomach upset'
is one euphemism I entirely approve of. Simon Ward (junior) will be late
'because we've overslept, Mr Sedgwick, I'm ever so sorry.'

8.25 'Can I put my little girl's name down for playschool?' (the nursery).

8.30 A call for the caretaker, who doubles as the LEA's keeper of camping
equipment.

8.34 A call about the majorette troupe (if that is the right word) that meets at the school on Monday and Friday evenings. I refer the caller to the parent who runs it, making a mental note to see how it's going, as, for reasons I'm not sure about, and for others I'd rather not own up to, I don't like majoretting. Nice kids become flouncy automatons as middle-aged gents look on . . .

8.40 A parent: Did I find Amanda's jumper? ' Sorry, I didn't.' 'It was almost new.' 'Sorry.' 'Well. It's a shame.' 'Yes it is.'

8.45 A parent: Is there swimming today? (Yes).

9.12 Valerie, a dinner lady who's been here thirteen years, rings to tell us she's leaving: 'My own kids are grown up now, I want a fuller job as I get bored in the school holidays.' She is going to the newsagent's down the road.

9.45 A parent: Sorry, but she forgot to tell us that her children are on holiday this week.

9.50 Wrong number.

9.55 Mrs Cowper, the new swimming instructor for the summer term, rang: a good omen, as she has the same name as the school. 'Is the pool working yet?' 'Yes.'

We missed some calls here: I was teaching, and Sue forgot to record them. Then:

11.00 A school in a different authority. The head wants to know about Lynda, who's applied for a post at his school: 'I'll send you a reference right away — .' 'Oh, thank you so much! But tell me now, what sort of person is she?'

I hate this situation. Why should I take the risk of one unconsidered noun of mine ('She is a good Methodist/amateur actress/poet/netball player') hindering a career (the head is, for example, a committed Anglo-Catholic who loathes Wesley and all his works; or he once sat through an amateur performance of *Waiting for Godot* that scarred his relations with drama groups for life)?

How can these things be decided on a casual phone-call? It does the children no favours, and the National Union of Teachers is right when it says that references should be open to the candidate; that therefore they cannot be telephoned. Headteacherly nudges across the country serve no interests except those of the heads making the call: 'Of course, she's a bit of a trouble-maker . . . he's heftily involved in the NAS . . . I wouldn't bother, if I were you, she can't organize . . . I don't know what you've got in mind, but I've found he'll do whatever's asked of him . . .'

Later in the term, the heads involved in Teacher Appraisal were to tell us that in future references will be based entirely on mutually agreed notes from teacher appraisal interviews. A good job, too: but what about all those careers, becalmed because of a casual word in a head's ear? What about those children who've missed the opportunity of the right teacher because of a head's personal opinion, about poets, maybe, or netball?

Indeed, this head asks me about Lynda's 'family stability'. 'Perfectly stable', I say. 'Has she got any children? . . .' The head goes on. Next time I'll be tougher at the beginning and refuse to say anything, but offer only the written reference.

A secondary deputy head rings: she sets out the agenda for her call: 'Three things, Fred . . .' I'm reminded of Baptist preachers, and mildly surprised that all her points don't begin with the same letter, for mnemonic reasons.

11.20 Adrian Wells (infant) is ill.

11.55-12.20 Phone closed to outside callers as Sue rings seven supply teachers for Lynda, who is on a theatre in education course on Friday. The seventh can do it.

12.50 pm The chairman rings. Can he go on a day trip with his son's class, and, if so, does he have to pay? Yes and no: if parents go, they're helping, and so have free places.

12.55 Julie, Head at Heath St Patrick's, rings, and I tell her that a head we both know, Ron, has got the job of headteacher appraiser. Julie: 'Well! Good heavens! Goodness! Good gracious! Well. Well.' I say that if he tries to appraise me, I'll slap his wrist: he once did an MEd thesis based on parent-teacher relations at Cowper, and when I said my principles were 'basically Christian and democratic', he wrote down 'Christian Socialist'. I mention this now merely as an example of the clock that struck thirteen: could you trust anything else he'd write, especially in the evaluation of teachers?

He also never let me see drafts of his work on the school: ownership of that data rested firmly in the researcher's camp. So I assume any appraisal information he might glean at Cowper would be his, or the authority's; not ours to use to make things better for the children; but theirs to use to check up on us.

2.00 There's been trouble at Sally's house. Grandma says would we make sure nobody except she or her husband, Sally's grandad, picks Sally up from school. Sally's mother has apparently beaten up her own father, and she and some friends have expelled the old couple, and are squatting in their home.

We failed to record any of the calls after this, because of the pressure of events. All I know for sure is that the goalkeeper dropped a few crosses, and the opponent's strikers had a festival afternoon.

Justin is now on diamorphine. This is, Janice tells me, a bad sign.

Press Release
There will be an exhibition of children's art from three local primary schools in the Burns Elliot Hall from 5 to 11 July this year.

There will also be work by three internationally known artists at the same exhibition. These artists spent seven days in March working with the children at the three schools . . . under the Arts Council's Artists in Schools scheme . . .

Emmanuel Jegede, who worked at Cowper School, is Nigerian. He is a poet, painter, sculpter and musician, and he helped the children to tell stories through carving in many different materials . . .

Rebecca Wallace, of the museum staff, and Fred Sedgwick of Cowper, are at the moment responsible for mounting the exhibition, which acknowledges the generous help of ————shire local education authority, ————ton City Council, and the Arts Council . . .

When the lower juniors came back from their trip to ——————, the adults' faces were hard and sad. Tim told me that one of the children had stolen a veteran's war medal from the museum. 'It has to be one of ours, we were the only school in the place . . . I suppose you could look on the bright side and note this is the first time this has happened to me in twenty years' teaching.' 'Me too', says Lynda, who's also done twenty years. 'And me.' I've been twenty years in the game too. We agreed to have a party at the end of the year.

I wrote to the parents, but we didn't recover the medal.

Dear Fred,
After much deliberation, I no longer wish to be considered for the acting deputy headship next term . . .

This was Lynda. The other applicants were Janice and Don, who both stuck it out to the last. Lynda said to me, 'I can't take the hassle — I don't mean the job, if I get it, but the bloody appointment process, the rivalry . . . I'd rather have nothing to do with it!'

Don is the youngish man who got married last Christmas. He has spent all his career at Cowper. Janice was 'head of infants' till the review and the whole-school approach got their grip on the place. Janice has taught secondary at some time in her career.

Over a couple of lunchtimes, I check on Damien and Mark, the terrorizers of Simon, and Margaret, Janey and Darren. I also look at Sam. There seems to be little fighting at lunchtimes at the moment, and the sexual activity is either nil or hidden. Stella seems to be eating well, too, despite being a proselytizing vegetarian.

A supply teacher we use a lot at Cowper sent her children to church school a long way from home. When I asked why, she said: 'It's nothing to do with education . . . or religion, come to that . . . it's other things, things like, well, at St James they have tablecloths at lunchtime, for example . . .'

Parents, whether they're teachers or not, often consider what the teacher counts as the real business of school — the educational conversation in the classroom — to be of secondary importance behind other issues that are often to do with social class: tablecloths at lunchtime, school uniforms, the manners of the children at the school, experienced once, perhaps, on a pavement while getting on a bus, and never to be forgotten. In 1987 I tripped painfully against one of these issues: crisps.

When I'd arrived, in 1984, there'd been a flourishing tuck shop, run by Sue and a team of fourth-year juniors. It made some £150 a year for school funds, selling nuts, crisps, raisins and biscuits at morning playtimes.

There were several things I disliked about it from the beginning of my time in the school: in ascending order, these were, first, the noisy queue that formed in the library each morning break; second, the chore infant teachers had of collecting 'tuck money'; third, the litter all over the premises, but most noticeably clogging the chain link fence that divides the school field from the houses in the royal crescents; fourth, the certainty that the shop numbed the children's appetite for lunch; and fifth, what was by then becoming a fasionable scare: the additives children were taking in with the crisps, most particularly tartrazine, the yellow dye that has been linked to hyperactivity.

Some mornings I watched 10-year-old Christopher, who was already obese, walk through the gates eating one packet of Walkers' crisps. He would then throw the paper away, and open another, like a chain smoker, almost oblivious of what he was doing. He had another packet from the tuck shop at playtime, and another in his lunchbox an hour later.

When I mentioned the possibility of at least closing up the supply of crisps from the school side, Sue said, 'We'll have to raise that £150 somehow', and Lynda asked, 'What about staff tuck?' So I did nothing for three years, my reform prey to my need to be thought a nice guy. Then in 1987 I wrote to the parents: 'From the beginning of next term there will be no tuck shop in school. Children should not bring in crisps and nuts, etc., but are welcome to bring in fruit to eat at the mid-morning break. The reasons for this change are . . .' There followed what I hoped was a parent-oriented version of the list given above.

Any number of announcements of educationally draconian implication would have caused less furore. Mrs Holt came to see me, and her comments will serve for others:

What right have you got to dictate what our children should eat? . . . Mine are going to go on bringing crisps whether you say they can or they can't . . . Mr Sedgwick, I'm not having it . . . You behave like a little Hitler, all the parents at the gate agree with me, they all say you've got no right to do this . . . When my Sean goes on bringing crisps to school, what will you do, take them away from him? . . . I'm taking him away to a school where the headmaster behaves in a reasonable manner . . . No, I'll look the numbers up for myself, thank you . . .'

In fact, only the three Holt children left, and they went to a school where crisps had never been allowed, where all children have to have two pairs of shoes, and where there is a forbidding list of school rules. The other parents calmed down. So did I. The issue fizzled away. Now, when you walk round the junior courtyard, you risk skidding on pieces of orange and banana skin.

But, of course, I had hopelessly mismanaged the affair, despite the fact that I was in the right — or maybe because of it. I should have told the governors what I was going to do. I could have let them get on with it, even to the point of getting the chairman to sign the letter. The office would gladly have sent in School Health to make the case for me. So I learned a management lesson: never act on your own unless you have to — which you rarely do.

It was a social issue, as I ruefully noted afterwards: a powerful representative (I'm seeing this now from the parents' point of view) of the middle classes trying to tell the less well-off about their children's diet, and by any standards, that's a bloody nerve. It was an educational issue, too, despite my earlier distinction. I'd taken on too complex a bundle with too simple a strategy, and I'll know better next time.

There's no response yet about the ladies' loos: we'll have to do something ourselves. One of the women says, 'You must get a man teacher next time you make an appointment, Fred', and a colleague responds, 'We don't need a man, we need a new lavatory — if you can tell the difference.'

There are toilets the children don't use. We'll re-designate them 'MEN' and 'WOMEN', though the dimensions are wrong.

A group of fourth year juniors are going to the Lake District soon with Don, Jeanette, Barbara, David the caretaker, and a group of parents. I am teaching some of them, and Hayley has written 'smove':

'Can you spell "smooth" right, please Hayley?'
'How do you spell it?'
Steven helps out: 's.m.o.o.t.h.'
Hayley: 'That's "soot"!'
[Uproar]

Each of the teachers who's going is preparing a different area of the curriculum, and, though I can't go, because the office won't give the right amount of supply cover, I'm doing the literature. To be lumbered with teaching Wordsworth to a group of 10/11-year-olds when you're not even going to taste the fruits is a hard fate, but, as Barbara says in her crisp style, 'There's Beatrix Potter as well, you know.'

I start off by making up some lines of my own about the rain that's pouring down outside, and which will, all too likely, have its equivalent in the Lakes next week:

> The first thing was
> we got wet
> but we didn't mind.
> Our parents grumbled
> and cars clogged the roads
> but we enjoyed the puddles
> and the wet-leaved branches
> that swung and scattered
> water in our faces
> like another, rougher,
> surprising christening;
> and the next thing
> was shouting, pulling,
> pushing boots off
> in the cloakroom;
> hanging things on hooks,
> leaving little lakes on the floor;
> and the last thing was
> Sir saying
> 'Write about the rain'
> and we wrote this . . .

Now get your data, I said. Research the rain. Some of them stood silent inside the dripping pollarded birch for a moment, while others dashed screaming across the playground in anoraks and boots. Others just sat in my room (where I'd started the session) and watched the rain run down the window.

> No birds are singing.
> When you look at the rain
> you feel a sense of smallness.
> Every slab of pavement
> changes its colour.
> The grass is helpless:
> it can't run and hide.

The raindrop settles on the top of the leaf and drips on the grass. It makes a silky skin . . . The tree trunk is holey. The rain pours down . . .

It feels smooth when it is on a leaf and it runs down the leaf and trickles off like a waterfall. The rain looks like a million specks of sand falling from the sky. The rain will cover everything in its sight.

The raindrops are little drums
when they hit the ground.
The leaf looks like it's been varnished.

The rain
hits the leaf
and squirms off
like a worm
leaving slime
all over the leaf . . .

Two of my interests come together here: poetry and research. Because what are children's poems if they aren't tiny research projects into the part of the world they're concerned with? They will check their findings with each other afterwards, thus 'triangulating' and 'pursuing discrepancies', to use two phrases from the ethnographic school of educational research. They are researching not only the world, but their own relationships with it; implicitly accepting an utter subjectivity that has become difficult for adults to understand. The children, however, know that the world is like this, because this is the language they can use when they write about it, after they have looked, looked and looked again.

A girl in Tim's lower junior class had got glue in her eye, but there was no bloodshot appearance. After bathing it, Sue sent her back to the classroom. Tim reported later that another girl had said, aghast and fascinated, 'Are you blind?' Danie brought her back. 'She can't see out of that eye.' The girl covered the other eye, Danie held up three fingers, and said: 'How many fingers?' The first girl, unhesitatingly: 'Four.'

Mrs Ferenz arrives to interview me on my view on primary management. After forty minutes she says, 'It's so refreshing to meet someone one totally agrees with . . . I've got an ulterior motive in coming here . . . I can tell you I'm the right person for your deputy headship . . .'

Job descriptions have never been my strong point, so I ran Reg at Hockney CP to ask what he'd written for his deputy headship. With minor alterations, I used his stuff:

Cowper County Primary School
Deputy Headship
The job description of a deputy head, like that of a head, is necessarily open-ended and, in many areas not specified below, the appointee will feel the need to take action from time to time. It is easier to outline the qualities which the deputy must have than to specify how they are to be used. Thus the deputy should be flexible and able to see the need to act in a whole range of contexts. The deputy must be sensitive to the needs of the other teachers, both as colleagues and as private individuals. S/he must be seen to be trustworthy and professional, so that colleagues will be able to be open in their relationship, confident that the deputy head has goodwill toward them within the context of the needs of the school. The deputy must be seen to be a successful class teacher and one who places great emphasis on the happiness and progress of the children. S/he must be efficient because, in a school of this size, the organization of time and other resources can be complex, especially in relation to the many special events and activities which take place. The deputy should be appropriately experienced so as to advise all staff on INSET needs and opportunities and professional development, should have kept abreast of some of the recent developments in the curriculum and should show awareness of the climate in which the educational process now takes place. S/he will be given every support in the further development of his/her professional understanding through following major courses and carrying out research within the school.

The successful applicant will help to develop further the lively curriculum at this large primary school. S/he will assist the head and a teacher who will already be in post with a C allowance in leading this development along the lines of the authority's curriculum papers, as adapted in terms of the National Curriculum and collaborative research carried out by teachers within the school.

Further development will be aimed at giving children greater autonomy, and at encouraging staff to reflect critically on their work.

There followed a list of some of the basic features of the job.

My notes after 'one of those days':

Two middle infant classes were out at the —————— Railway, a good eighty minute trip away. Sixty juniors, plus four staff and five parents, were in the Lakes. I was teaching full-time the third and fourth years who hadn't gone and a few second years.

The day with these children began with swimming. As Mrs Cowper, the instructor, worked with them, I watched, and planned the rest of the morning's work in detail: I'd already decided that the swimming itself was too strong a stimulus to miss, taking place as it did at the very beginning of the day. They would draw themselves and their friends in the pool, after looking at some reproductions of David Hockney paintings. Then they would write descriptions of the feeling of being in or under the water.

But when I came out of the pool with the lank-haired kids, all apparent Brylcream and genuine talcum power, I met a problem. The middle infants' coach hadn't turned up. A misunderstanding or an administrative cock-up? . . . The children were sitting about in the sun with their teachers and parents, some ten or twelve, who were going on the trip as well. I felt the managerial soft belly of the school was uncomfortably exposed . . .

The coach firm said they could get a coach to us, but not for another half hour. And they couldn't get the children back till 6.00 (it should have been 3.30). I worried about it for a minute, then decided they should go. Then I found Sue had already anticipated this decision with the coach firm.

In fact, the coach didn't turn up till 10.45. Then, at 12.45, Gillian, one of the teachers, rang: The driver had got lost and they'd only just arrived.

While I worked with the swimming group, Sue was ringing round to tell the infants' parents that the children would be late back from their trip, and some were, of course, proving elusive. One of these was Mrs Browne, the assailant in the fight this book begins with. Social Services wouldn't give us the number of the Women's Refuge, but they agreed to telephone with the message that Christina would be late back to school after her day out. I also left a message at the hotel (euphemism for hostel) where her homeless estranged husband lives, because it wasn't clear which parent had custody. Then, as far as this family was concerned, we hoped for the best.

At teatime, Sue and some teachers went round to the houses we'd not been able to contact, and left notes in the letter boxes. The rest of the day had gone well, with work everywhere following up the lower juniors' trip and the swimming session, and that mysterious quiet in the four vacant classrooms. I went to a meeting at 4.00, leaving the deputy to greet the trippers. 'It was great', said the teachers, having, apparently, forgotten the administrative details that had left them stranded at school and in the coach for far longer than anyone with normal patience would have tolerated.

But five of the parents weren't so happy: 'I don't think it was worth the money', said one. 'Come to Friday's assembly and see the work they do.'

Aaron, a behaviour problem last term — tipping up benches, knocking friends about, defying dinner ladies — has calmed down. His hair has grown from neo-fascist crop to potential hippy, and his writing has become free-wheeling. Mum, whose marriage broke up six months ago, seems easier-going too. Maybe Aaron is coming to terms with the new state of affairs? Or perhaps he is learning to play the school game?

The Chairman hints occasionally that my reports to the governors (one side of A4) are too short. So I've gone for the jackpot with this term's:

Sometimes one wonders what the function of this report is. It is well-known that long reports can be used to blind with science, to pull the wool over lay eyes. On the other hand, short reports may lead to suspicions on the part of lay people that things are being hidden from them. A balance between the two positions must be attained, with the knowledge in the forefront of our minds that, first, governors have far greater responsibilities coming their way for statutory reasons, and, second, governors at this school have traditionally taken a genuine interest in the children's learning for which I, for one, am grateful. It is to be hoped that this will continue.

In curricular terms, the most significant developments since the last meeting have been in maths. It was a great disappointment to us all that only 7 per cent of the children were represented at the open evening arranged in March. But, nevertheless, it was a splendid evening for those who did find the time to attend. During the days previously, I'd spent a good deal of time canvassing parents, and it was probably this work and similar work done by colleagues — time-consuming, it has to be said, and not entirely unembarrassing — that probably raised the attendance from a derisory 2 or 3 per cent. The parents who did come engaged in lively dialogue with the County Maths Adviser (whose help I greatly appreciate) and with teachers. Jean Drew is to be congratulated on setting up such an entertaining and educational evening. My thanks also go to my colleagues who set up their stalls on Maths and Art, Maths on TV, computers, place value, geometry, Maths and Music, and calculators.

The governors will already know about work in science, as they were given a splendid presentation by Tim Kite at the last meeting. Work in this area of the curriculum has been growing apace recently, and any reputation the school may have in certain quarters of being biassed towards the arts — music, painting and poetry in particular — is demonstrably unfair. Nevertheless, one of the most exciting experiences I have ever had in a school was the residence here in March of the Yoruba poet, painter, draughtsman, sculptor and musician Emmanuel Jegede. If governors are interested in a fuller description of this remarkable seven days, I would refer them to an article in *The Times Educational Supplement* which demonstrates, in literary and photographic terms, the richness of the experience twenty-eight children in the school had as a result of our spending some of our GRIST money on this project . . . Emmanuel placed centre stage (where, notwithstanding their sidelining in certain powerful quarters these days, they should be) the arts, that help children to discover themselves, the world around them, and the relationship, complex and difficult as it is, between them. Emmanuel's work was also an opportunity to present the children with that rare thing that today's world all too easily hides: beauty.

Work in music has developed too, as Lynda has used extra GRIST money to help the less musically able teachers to develop their work in this area. It has been a delight, in particular, to watch young infants gain some purchase on the basic skills of instrument-making.

This money came from another area of —————shire. I was placed, for four days, in a residency in and around ————————— as a writer in residence. The schools there paid us enough money for four days' supply cover, and we used it to free Lynda from her class to develop the music outlined above . . .

The buzz phrase at the moment is 'whole-school', as we work towards a greater coherence in teaching styles and the ways in which children are helped to learn. Much credit for this improvement in our professionalism must go to Barbara Myers and Janice Marks, who are currently on a course run by the Institute of Education. Their studies are enabling teachers here to examine their practice collaboratively, and have given rise to excellent work in music, the social and political aspects of the curriculum (led here by Charlotte Pugh, who now has responsibility for this sadly neglected area) and, next, multicultural education.

Staff meetings take place every month, when we inform each other about plans for future teaching . . .

There is also exciting development in computer-assisted learning, as children, especially young children, gain experience on the new Nimbus computer with some of the Art programs. We are, though, desperately short on computers: three among 360 children is a ridiculous shortfall.

This report so far has concentrated on the vital aspect of the school (or despite occasional appearances to the contrary, any school): that is, the educational relationship that exists between the children and the teacher. But it should also be noted by governors that there are other educational aspects to a school — namely, those that exist between the adults. In this school, teachers are constantly involved in in-service work . . . They are taught, and they teach . . . It is important that this education should extend to the other adults in the school: parents and governors, who also have a role to play, first in educating themselves in the way school has changed over the past years; and, second, in educating us in the external realities in which they are involved, and which impinge on our school and its functions . . .

We continue to receive visitors to see work here . . . (there follows a list of teachers, social workers, health visitors, journalists and photographers). Articles about the school appear regularly in *The Times Educational Supplement* and *Art and Craft,* and governors should see me if they want to see this work . . . Staff continue to run fund-raising discos for the children . . .

If there have been disappointments, they sometimes involve parents. It should be reported to the governors that abuse of children of one kind or another is increasingly a concern of the staff, and that two of us have attended case conferences on particular children in the last two months. The drop-in has declined . . . The PTA still depends on a very small number of willing hands . . . Nevertheless, one of the joys of this job is watching parents regularly help children with their work; not merely cleaning paintpots, or listening to readers, but doing exciting tasks throughout the school. I am grateful that these parents are so keen to inform themselves of the realities of life in school at first hand . . .

Staffing

We congratulate:

Don Snaid on his achievement of the degree of BEd.

Donna West on her being accepted on a part-time BPhil course.

The deputy head on his appointment to a headship. We recognize his contribution to Cowper School, and thank him for it.

We are sorry that Susie Latimer, classroom ancillary, is leaving us, as her family moves to Hull. We wish her well.

We are sorry that Jeanette Belway-Smith, who has made such an exemplary start to her career, is leaving us. We wish her well, too.

We seek to confirm the appointment of Miss Helena Johns of St Arthur's School, made by the chairman, the schools' adviser, and me.

We need to appoint internally, before September, an acting deputy head, and, for January 1989, a permanent one.

We also seek to confirm the appointment of Barbara Myers to a C allowance from September this year. This appointment, to assist the school in the implementation of the National Curriculum, was also made by the chairman, an adviser, and me.

We were also able to appoint a summer reception teacher, Mrs Anna Verity-Brown.

Miss Watkins will hold a temporary A allowance next year, and will be responsible for bringing out three issues of a magazine of children's work.

There is writing here I'd never normally commit. Long words like 'notwithstanding' are there for ballast only, and passive constructions like 'It is to be hoped . . .' and 'A balance . . . must be attained . . .' are there to dehumanize, to fit the stuff of a school's life to a managerial perspective. Gross trendyisms, such as 'engage in lively dialogue' and 'shortfall' can only be justified (and that barely) as jokes. Similarly, the quaint archaism 'growing apace', and that amazing question-begging use of the word 'beauty' can only be seen as patronizing.

Sue and I went to visit Justin. We told ourselves in the car not to say 'How are you?' He was lying in bed in the living room, puffy around the face and, when he stood up, uncertain on his feet. Ben said, 'Come and see me be a monkey on the climbing frame.' He took Justin's toys and pleaded, in different ways, for our attention. Then Sue and I talked with Justin, about watches and television. Sue said, as we went back to school, 'That's the hardest thing I've ever done.'

I signed a passport application for Nicky, who was going to visit her father in America.

The following account of the Lakes trip is made up from notes by parents, children, teachers . . . and me, left behind at Cowper:

MONDAY:
I felt envious as I watched them gather round the coach. After farewells at 8.00 . . .

. . . We set off for Buttermere [a parent, Joy, writes]. There was a lot of chatter and exuberance, and also some pale, subdued faces. Gradually all the children relaxed enough to enjoy the journey. But it was a very hot day, and Jeanette became the lady of the buckets as she ministered to the sick.

The children seemed to have mixed ideas about the forthcoming events. The general feeling was that they were on a day trip, and that the coach would be turning round soon and heading back to those comfortingly named roads: Princess, Cowper, St George's, Windsor, Hanover, Unwin . . . It was unreal for them that they would actually be sleeping with friends hundreds of miles from anyone familiar. 'I was more scared than excited', admitted Gemma: 'Sometimes you want to get away from home, but you miss them, don't you?' 'Will we get there today or will we have to sleep on the coach', asked Darren, a boy whose short fuse worried the teachers. How would he be far from home? . . .

. . . Barbara [I interrupt here] had had enough faith in him to take him, despite the times he'd knocked other children about, or run blindly out of school, or yelled in a rage at everyone about him . . .

. . . When we arrived [Barbara noted] the childrren talked about television, especially the Nelson Mandela concert in the news that week . . .

. . . I interrupt: I was pleased to hear from Don that evening. I put a message on a blackboard outside the front door of the school: ALL WELL. ARRIVED SAFELY. WEATHER SUPERB. LOVE TO ALL — THE LAKES PARTY. WATCH THIS SPACE FOR MORE NEWS TOMORROW . . .

TUESDAY:

. . . I am sitting [wrote a parent the next evening] in the lounge of the hostel, on the first floor. It is 9.00, but broad daylight, and amazingly lovely as I glance up and see the green hills and the mountains through the large window. Sheep baa and move around on the other side of the dry stone wall.

I am not alone. With me are a dozen or more showered and unshowered children with lowered heads, diligently trying to apply themselves to sketches and resumes of the day's events. Some are in nightware, having been the lucky ones to have made use of the two showers available for females, and the two for males. Some are still sweaty in their dayclothes.

Yesterday's soup — an interesting green colour — is referred to as 'asparaguts' by my table and 'sheepdip' by Don's. On today's trip round Lake Windermere, someone commented, '£75 just to walk round a field!' On passing a postcard shop, Mel pointed out a view of Windermere: 'Oh Miss — just like Municipal Park!'

Already the bedding used by the hostel has a new name. It consists of a continental quilt, a pillow, and a cotton item which is rather like a sleeping bag lining. The children call them 'hot dogs'. One of us asked the resident staff for 'another hot dog', only to be given a what-on-earth-are-you-talking-about look. It then dawned on us: 'hot dog' was an invention, evidence of the unofficial creativity of children left alone for a while to live their lives together . . .

. . . LAKES PARTY ALL WELL. IT'S VERY HOT AND SUNTANS ARE COMING ON. LOVE TO ALL PARENTS.

WEDNESDAY:

. . . Another misunderstanding . . .

Don wrote: The highlight of the day for me was seeing a dipper in a stream we crossed... It was jumping in and swimming underwater as they amazingly do, and re-emerging further down the stream. The children with me just wandered on, much to my disgust: they couldn't see it. Then, as I talked to Stella, I realised they were looking for a fish. We spent ten minutes watching the dipper then. Later I was comforted by the fact that they saw a buzzard on top of Rannerdale Knotts . . .

. . . Today [a parent wrote] most of us climbed our first mountain. I was pleasantly surprised at the generous width of the path zigzagging its way up, and relieved to find the ascent well within our novice capabilities. David the caretaker was with the group as an experienced walker, and carried a soft rope, a stove and a rucksack. He was most encouraging about distances and timing: we were within schedule. But it was constantly discouraging when the four of us bringing up the rear reached each stopping point as the vanguard set off again. Nevertheless, we deliberately placed one walking boot in front of another, and, panting with effort, open-mouthed, reached the height of 1160 feet. An enormous cheer went up as a stone was placed on the cairn. 'I didn't know', said Allan, 'you could get so high.' David the caretaker brewed up some tea. 'Sir', said Allan, 'I think your beard grows more quickly in the sun.'

. . . Another angle on the first climb came from Martin, who wrote that evening: After about an hour me and half the people were tired out. My climbing boots were weighing my feet down. When we stopped a second time to have our lunch we had to do some drawing and some writing. I drawed Crummock Lake. I was looking at the view as I jumped on to a ledge. I lost my balance and fell down another little ledge. I wasn't hurt even though David thought I was. About five minutes later we set out for the top. Mrs Peters and the others who couldn't make it stayed behind. When we got to the top we put a stone there. At the top I took my last photo. We could see Crummock Water and Buttermere Lake. We stayed at the top for half an hour and then we had to come down. A little way down we stopped for a game of rounders. It was boys stick girls. The boys won. At about 4.30 we stopped off at Crummock Water. Some people went in paddling but me and some others were doing skimmers. I got the highest {number of skimmers], nine. When we stopped at Buttermere village, Miss went into the shop and bought everyone an ice lolly. I bought some mint cake for my brother Ian . . .

Don said later, 'Some of the children seemed completely lost up the mountain: "Sir, there's no roads, no houses, no shops, there's nothing here".'

. . .THE LAKES PARTY ARE WELL AND TIRED AFTER A DAY CLIMBING. THEY ARE ALL BEHAVING AND LOOKING FORWARD TO SEEING YOU ON FRIDAY . . .

THURSDAY:

The parent writes again: All is quiet except for the birds, and the sound of water, and the odd child forgetting that this is a period of work. Barbara was talking a moment ago about the contrast between this and where the children live: this green, airy meadow, and roads with no places to play. 'I'm going to take photographs of this so no one forgets this moment.' Margaret, who, the teachers tell me, is in all kinds of trouble at school, is behaving perfectly, gazing in wonder at everything she sees. A local Catholic charity paid the £75 for her to come.

Barbara says there probably won't be a journey next year, because schools can't claim VAT back anymore, and, even more significantly, they won't be allowed, under new legislation, to charge for journeys. It surely can't be deliberate, can it, this taking away from children who have so little travel what travel they have?

They had a ride this morning in an open carriage on the narrow guage railway that runs between Eskdale and Ravenglass. I had forgotten about the smuts! Now Neil is writing in his notebook:

Here comes a train
racing along
faster than lightning
if I'm not wrong.
It starts to slow down
into the station.
Everyone's pushing
their friend's relation.
Boarding the train
with so much speed
my helpless shouts
they do not heed . . .

The field is littered with butercups and ferns. Flies buzz around the bent heads of the children. The adults walk about them, pencils in hand . . .

. . . THE LAKES PARTY WISH YOU WERE THERE. WATCH THIS SPACE FOR ESTIMATED TIME OF ARRIVAL TOMORROW . . .

FRIDAY:

. . . 'Why is Mr Walne whistling down the phone?' His dog, at home, had snaffled his wife's slippers, and wouldn't give them back unless told to do so by Mr Walne . . .

Joy: Lots of buzz and activity, last minute packing, tracing lost articles, odd socks and unclaimed underwear hastily collected together. Less hearty breakfasts being eaten. Travel sickness pills issued. Suitcases handed to Terry the driver. The predictable group photo, the gradual shuffle to get everyone in. Then the photo of the four members of the hostel staff — young, good natured, in touch with the humour and fun of the children. One of them had emerged from the serving hatch the previous evening and squirted a nicely executed rosette in cream on the bald patch of Phil, one of the parents.

. . . THE LAKES PARTY HAVE LEFT: ETA 6.30 PM. WATCH THIS BOARD FOR CHANGES . . .

We're off. I loved it all: the sheer friendliness of the children, the feeling of being wanted all the time: 'Will you sit with us, Miss?' Mel had put on her cleanest clothes, and packed her suitcase perfectly, in readiness for seeing her family again, while Sarah couldn't find any clothes even remotely clean. After dressing, she threw everything else into her case, saying it didn't matter what she wore, her mum and dad would be pleased to see her anyway. I bet she was right, too.

    . . . THE LAKES PARTY WILL BE TWO HOURS LATE OWING TO HOLD-UPS ON THE MOTORWAY. ALL WELL AND IN GREAT SPIRITS . . .

In fact, they were three hours late, and back at school we made tea for the waiting mothers, fathers, brothers and sisters.

    Barbara wrote, much later, about a week 'crammed with children, their demands, needs, etc., suddenly disappeared . . . an empty playground and my mind screaming with the silence . . .' Don pointed out to me, as the children went bubbling home with their smiling families: 'Nobody's come to meet Margaret. She didn't want to go home. "I wish I was still in the Lake District", she said.'

It had been agreed meanwhile to convert two of the children's loos to staff use.

A Friday assembly. Lots of writing, drawing and painting stemming from the infant's trip. A parent says to me, 'I see what you mean about the value of the trip now.' Another says, 'I still don't think it was worth the money . . . those assemblies are just a front . . .'

I don't know for sure whether I'll ever be able to use the following notes. But I go on making them, anyway:

> Justin is in a bad way, his face puffy and pale, his speech slow and sometimes slurred. Janice had arranged a visit from the Police Liaison Officer and a dog (with a handler), and Justin's mother had brought him in specially, pushing him along in a baby's buggy: 'I'm a king, I go about on a throne!' Everyone — teachers, police officers, children — gathers round him as he strokes the dog.
>
> After a while, he has to go home because he is feeling tired. Roy says, 'See you tomorrow Justin.' His mother says he was getting bored at home, so I run to my room to grab a pile of books to lend him. Sue fetches a spare copy of the infants' photograph. Then the nursery teacher and a few parents come to say 'Hello', all trying not to say 'How are you?' because it's obvious.
>
> Mother and son laugh and smile at everyone. He has two watches, and he likes my new one, which cost me £9.99, and which has a transparent face, so you can see the works. He tells me he can count to

ten in German, and he does so. His mother wheels him back to the
house, where his father is busy on the extension.

SPECIAL AREAS OF TEACHING INTEREST AND EXTRA-
CURRICULAR CONTRIBUTIONS:
Renaissance Education — a wholesome total approach to run through
the whole curriculum. The true integration of arts and sciences and the
real development of the individual evolving into a caring, questioning,
sensitive human via the creative exploration and study of art; music;
poetry; sciences; dance etc.
PERSONAL INTERESTS:
In ascending order of importance: Astro-physics; Beekeeping; Philoso-
phy; Children.
 . . . it is the narrowness, selfishness, minuteness of sensations
that you have to deplore . . . It is vital that individuals' strengths are
utilised . . . throughout the organic network of valued individualism
 . . . Pericles described true education to be citizens excelling in
versatility, resourcefulness and physical self-reliance . . . (we must be)
unblinkered by compartmentalisation. A vesicular approach only
encourages narrow, fragile vulnerability, whereas the robust form of
questioning, caring, individualistic, personal education can weather
the storms of intolerance and the doldrums of complacency . . .'

— from Mrs Ferenz's application for the deputy headship.

Junior sports day was bright for a change. We always make the runners in the
obstacle race struggle up the overgrown bank by Cowper Close, spluttering and
complaining, before they go through the usual hoops, or under the usual canes,
or over the usual hurdles. As Margaret and Danielle arrived at an obstacle
together, Danielle said politely: 'After you.' Don (in charge of the morning)
said to 7-year-old Lee: 'Which house are you in?' '17 Unwin Close.'
   I remember my tutor at college, who'd been a commissioned officer in the
army. He'd once ordered a troup of private soliders, laden with haversacks, after
a day's march, to wade through a cold, muddy stream, and one of them had said
'No'. My tutor had reflected afterwards on the pointlessness of his order: how
'No' was the only sane response. I felt much like that on sports day: 'Don't run
across that track! . . . Don't stand on your seats! . . . Don't boo!' 'Why not?'
'Because it's dangerous, impolite and rude.' But a day when I'm not dangerous,
impolite and rude I count as a day wasted.
   I pondered all this while I watched two parents, high-heeled, attractive in
what a Kingsley Amis character once called 'a taut-bloused sort of way', gallop
like lame gazelles across the track. What should I yell at them, students of the
Bonsall campus?
   I never like being starter. That day I was hopelessly sweaty, inelegant,

unheadteacherly, on stage in front of all these people, many of whom believe that what I do is less than their children are worthy of. Give 'em the basic skills, Mrs Jameson is thinking, as she holds her Silk Cut behind her ear. All this scribble scribble scribble is all very well, but . . . Or there's Mrs Furnival, wondering how many jumpers her Amanda and Samantha have lost at this school. Or Mrs Smith-Wesson, guessing, I bet HE has a Jammy Dodger, or a packet of Hula-hoops with *his* coffee . . .

The reds won. They always do. Two fourth years came and collected the shield from me, and the parents clapped. Mrs Scott, whose Gemma is leaving this term, said to me as we walked back to school, 'Thank you for all you and your staff have done for Gemma . . . I'm grateful your educational path crossed hers, Mr Sedgwick.'

Dear Mrs Hurst,
Mark was in rather a messy state today, as a result of not cleaning himself properly after going to the toilet. I didn't let him go swimming for obvious reasons. This has been happening rather a lot lately and the smell is not pleasant. The children also notice and call him names.

Maybe we could discuss this matter further as Mark is finding it very embarrassing. Could you make an appointment to see me?
Yours sincerely

L M Noah (teacher)

Midday. Margaret brings me a drawing of a kestrel. 'I liked it in the Lakes . . . can I go again next year?' Then ten minutes later she's in trouble. A dinner lady has asked her to 'sit there, Margaret' and Margaret wants to sit elsewhere. Neither side can back down, because of losing face, and Margaret is brought to me. 'Why can't you just do what you're told, what the others do, Margaret?' Hands folded across chest, defiant look out of window. 'Why not?' No change. 'Margaret, why not?' And then, of course, I lose my temper.

The children at Cowper eat their lunches off plastic airline trays, first course at one end, sweet at the other. Most of the children eating the meals are getting them free, while the others bring packed lunches. A very small number go home.

Here comes Jeremy, age 7, holding his tray. It's full of spaghetti bolognese — innocent, though, of onion and garlic — and bakewell tart. He also has a plastic cup full of milk-shake and half an apple. Jeremy can do something like 0-8 mph between the hatch and the table allotted to him, where he doesn't want to go. 'Miss!' he wails in a long set of about three drawn-out syllables. 'Jeremy', I say in three crisp ones, and he sits down.

Later the children ask, 'Can I turn?' (the tray round) and 'Can I scrape?' There is very little waste, because there is a choice, and the cooking is sound. It can be noisy though. But it's worse when the packed lunches have come in, swinging their plastic boxes marked with little ponies and he-men, and cracking them down on the tables, so it sounds like sporadic machine gunfire has broken out. Loud conversation ensues about who's got what. One boy surreptitiously shakes his can of Fanta under the table, and innocently asks Miss to open it. She is not amused. Other children trade Applause bars for Milky Ways.

Jeremy is carrying his empty tray at a relatively restrained pace. I ask: 'What are you going to call the baby, Jeremy?' 'Megatron.' He drops his cutlery in the bowl, places his tray on the pile, and makes for the door . . . Minutes later, he's made the playground. If this were winter, he'd have fastened his coat by one button under his chin, letting the rest of it splay out like Superman's cloak. Now, though, he has to use his imagination. He zaps a couple of bystanders, who ignore him. He tears off, bumping into other boys who shout at him crossly.

The rest of the scene through the classroom window looks like a cover for an Opie book. Here's a skipping game, there's a group of younger children, all trying to hold the dinner lady's hand. Another group have draped themselves over the dome-shaped climbing frame, and are dropping into the sandpit at the base of it. Other children just talk in groups.

Four boys are standing in a corner formed by two walls. 'What have they been doing?' 'Fighting, and when I tell them to stop they won't.' I take this sheepish group to my room, and write their names down on a piece of paper, and pin it to my wall. 'Do you want your name off my wall?' 'Yes.' 'Then behave all this week at dinner times, and it comes down . . . if you mess Mrs Spenser about again, I'll ring home. Do you understand?' 'Yes.' 'You'd better stay in today, as you've started so badly . . .' I look along the row: three of them are from one-parent families.

Margaret: 'What do you want me to say? . . . (Nobody under 24 has ever said this to me before now.) 'You all hate me here, you treat me as a poor girl . . .'

At 1.00, I send the fighting infants out, telling the dinner lady to bring them to me if they don't behave. I'd recovered my temper with Margaret within seconds of losing it and was feeling guilty: 'We don't hate you, Margaret, in fact the opposite . . . There's a lot of people here who care a lot about you . . . I'm sorry, though, I lost my temper with you . . . Can you be calm now?' 'Yes.' 'Go and have your lunch, then go out to play, and if anything gets you down — see me.' 'Yes Sir.'

Later, to a dinner lady: 'How's Margaret been?' 'Fine. Fine . . . good as gold . . .'

The conventional view of headship, fostered by the National Association of Headteachers, is that pressures on heads are unremitting. Indeed, there are times when four or five serious things are happening at once. You're a football manager whose goalkeeper has resigned, whose central defenders are mostly injured, and whose crowds are declining. And there is the atmosphere: for the football manager, it emanates from the crowd. For the headteacher, it comes largely from Government's nags, threats . . . and its reams of bad prose.

I often feel the opposite of a prostitute: she has power without responsibility, while I have responsibility without power. Or: why is a headteacher like a mushroom? Because they keep you in the dark and every now and then someone comes in and throws a load of shit over you.

Not many people apply for headships. But there are times when the pressure suddenly lifts . . .

It's nine o'clock on a Friday morning. All the staff are in, as they nearly always are. I don't have to worry about assembly till this afternoon, and I'd finished the post by 8.45: mostly, it went in the bin. Two phone calls and three letters were all it required. No parents wanted to see me, so I'm doing my tour early . . .

Lynda's lower junior class is in the nursery, working alongside half the 4-year-olds. Lynda herself, who prides herself on being able to make any pre-school child yell at fifty yards, is holding a 3-year-old on her knee, and Samantha, one of the juniors, says admiringly, 'Mrs Noah's just stopped her crying.' Other juniors are remembering the good times: playing with sand and water, talking to the young ones: getting in ten minutes of experience that is valuable to them in many ways.

They are experiencing young children. They are realizing that school life on a Friday morning is more than sums and writing. They are meeting other adults: parents and nursery nurse, who have different perspectives on the world. They are seeing their teacher in a new light.

As they walk back to their more usual curriculum, at 9.20, I go with them as far as their classroom, and then on to the swimming pool, where Charlotte is with the other half of the nursery children. Some parents are in the pool — four mothers, and a father who is evidently very impressed with Mrs Cowper. The children have placebo armbands on — these have very little physical effect, but build up confidence. The father gazes cow-like at the busy instructor. Three children complete a width. Another six are being rubbed down and talcum'd in the changing rooms. One tiny girl is resolute about her refusal to progress beyond the middle of the footbath.

In the infant general purpose area, two classes are singing, with public bar gusto, 'I saw a mouse (where?) there on the stair . . .'; and up the corridor a whole class of juniors is playing Battleships in groups of five or six, learning about co-ordinates.

To describe the display screens of the school at this stage of the school year is encouraging. Relationships between groups of children and teachers have surmounted (for the most part) difficulties, and now generate fresh-looking work.

In the deputy's classroom, for example, there is a wall-sized picture made from tissue paper (the water) and sugar paper (the swimmers) of the bath during a lesson. The tissue paper doesn't offer any evidence of children being used on a production line — no screwed-up balls; it is spread, and the dye from one colour mixes in the paste with the dye from another. The human figures have been cut out round the children's bodies, as they imitated breast-stroke, crawl or butterfly.

On another wall there are some striking Matisse pastiches: these 6-year-olds had been looking at the draughtsmanship by scissors of his late period. The work is obviously inspired, or informed by, the artist: but the shapes are the children's own. There is no hint of template — either in art, or in the broader sense: children are not being given grids into which they must fit their thinking . . .

No, that is sentimental: we do give children conceptual templates all the time, and my treatment of Margaret is an example. But perhaps there is less evidence of that than in some places.

In Janice's room there is an atmosphere that suggests that at any moment teacher, children or parents might discover something they didn't know before. All have their heads down as I walk through the door. There are pictures on the walls done in many media: burst bubbles, ink and card; torn strips of paper; the ubiquitous close observation, but done boldly, in thick-nibbed felt-tip pen, and charcoal — in this case of a dead pheasant the teacher had picked off the road.

There are also pictures that belong to the teacher, flower arrangements and bits of machinery salvaged from wrecked cars seen on a Sunday afternoon walk. Defunct starter motors, ignition switches, radiator grills and even gearboxes travel round the building from time to time, to be played with, drawn, written about, discussed. Art? Writing? Science? I often can't label this kind of work, but hope that there'll be room for it when the National Curriculum has landed on us.

In the hall, there are fourteen large paintings/collages on the high wall, one contributed by each class. This term they are on a journey theme. You can tell which groups of children have more control over their pictures, which have less, by the quality of the shape and colour: if the teacher has put too much of him/herself in, there's a certain expectedness about the final product.

Some teachers claim they lose sleep over this task, every time the notice is put up in the staffroom by Lynda:

BIG PICTURES NEXT TERM
ON COLOUR
by 24 SEPTEMBER PLEASE
Please state now what size/shaped boards you want, and give some idea
of what colour you want.

Next to this notice is a reproduction of Delacroix's 'Liberty on the Barricades'. Someone has stuck a bubble coming out of bare-bosomed, tricolor-waving Liberty's mouth: 'It's murder getting a trolley in Tesco's on a Friday evening.'

My room is next door, and when I glance in, I find the internal post has arrived: so that's the end of the tour. I sit at my desk.

Among the usual job circulars, advertisements for exhibitions, concerts and dances, lists of courses and computer printouts about capitation, there's a letter about teacher appraisal marked in the margin with three dots ('for action'); a ten-page enclosure about school reviews (inspections) and the changes that are going to take place there; a letter headed 'CHILD ABUSE: a response is required from all schools'; material about the election of parent-governors (we need two more next term following current legislation); an invitation to submit applications for secondment (shall I bother this year?) and a letter from the office on 'enterprise education'. Apparently this is not political, but peace studies is. Maybe the NAHT is right after all.

But I did teach that afternoon. It was bright, and I got a group of older juniors to walk with me under the trees beyond Don's room, and to write 'To the Sun':

> You are a cat's eye gleaming in the dark sky.
> Your beams are water sprinklers spraying out.
> You are a birthmark to the universe.
> The sky is a dark room,
> you are its only lightbulb.
> Your rays are streams of light
> bursting from beneath the clouds.
> You are an eagle flying through the sky
> like a flying electric blanket.
> You share your heat with the world.
> You are a pond of light.
> The earth is just one of the planets
> full of fish
> you have to care for.

This work — not a poem, but notes towards one — stems from a walk and readings of Akenaten's 'Hymn to the Sun' and Philip Larkin's poem, 'Solar'. I don't mind how far-fetched the children's images are: I often say to them, 'I'd sooner your writing was strange than true.' The object is to help them make themselves into thinkers who can interpret the world for themselves, in their own terms.

Art is always about creating something new, never about recording perceptions other people have had. It is better to take risks, to sound silly, maybe, than to use, in Barthes' words, 'the conformist, plagiarizing edge' of language that gets us nowhere. Such plagiarizing, not only in the literal sense of stealing lines, but even more so in Barthes' sense, is evident in the entries to national poetry competitions for young people, and it is essentially a conservative template. Art, on the other hand, reaching forward to discovery, is potentially subversive, and always questioning.

I suppose our elders and betters know that, and that's why the arts come so far behind maths, science and instrumental English in the National Curriculum.

A longish tradition at Cowper dictates that, at the end of the summer term, there is a leavers' service. The children from the third years downward sing songs for the fourth years; or put on a play, or dance, or play instruments. Then a VIP presents the leavers with a small gift (paid for by the PTA) and makes a speech. This year, it was Lynda's idea to ask Stuart Murdoch of Watford FC. He arrived in a smart charcoal suit, with a maroon tie marked 'WATFORD' on the bottom, and gulped a mug of sweet, milky coffee. The least shy man I have ever known, his old charm was unaffected by relegation.

It was a steaming July afternoon. I sat next to Stuart as the children sang. 'You're sweating, mate', he said. 'You ought to get some jogging in.' After the concert, Stuart presented each leaver with a group photograph. As the children came up to us one by one, I tried to whisper something about them in Stuart's ear: 'Good cellist . . . Plays a good game of football . . . Good at painting . . . Only came to us last term . . .' He always used this information. Then he made a speech, about Elton John, football and journeys: his from headteaching to Watford, the children's from Cowper to high school:

> And it isn't true that the second years put your heads down the toilets
> — it wasn't true when I was at school, it wasn't true even when you
> were at school, was it Mr Sedgwick? . . . I was a bit worried about my
> journey to Vicarage Road, and I think you're all probably a bit worried
> about your journey to high schools, even if you pretend you're not
> [nods from parents]. But it will be OK, if you do what you know, what
> Cowper has taught you, is right . . .

Afterwards, impressed by Stuart's link with their parents' hero Elton John, they crowded round him for his autograph.

Notice in the staffroom:

> Acting deputy next term: Janice Marx. Interviews for the permanent
> deputy headship, last week in September.

On another hot evening, the art adviser opened the exhibition at the Burns Elliot Hall. Emmanuel came too, and *The Star* and *The Advertiser* took photographs.

Then Jeanette, the classroom ancillary and the deputy left in a flood of wine. And the summer holidays were really here.

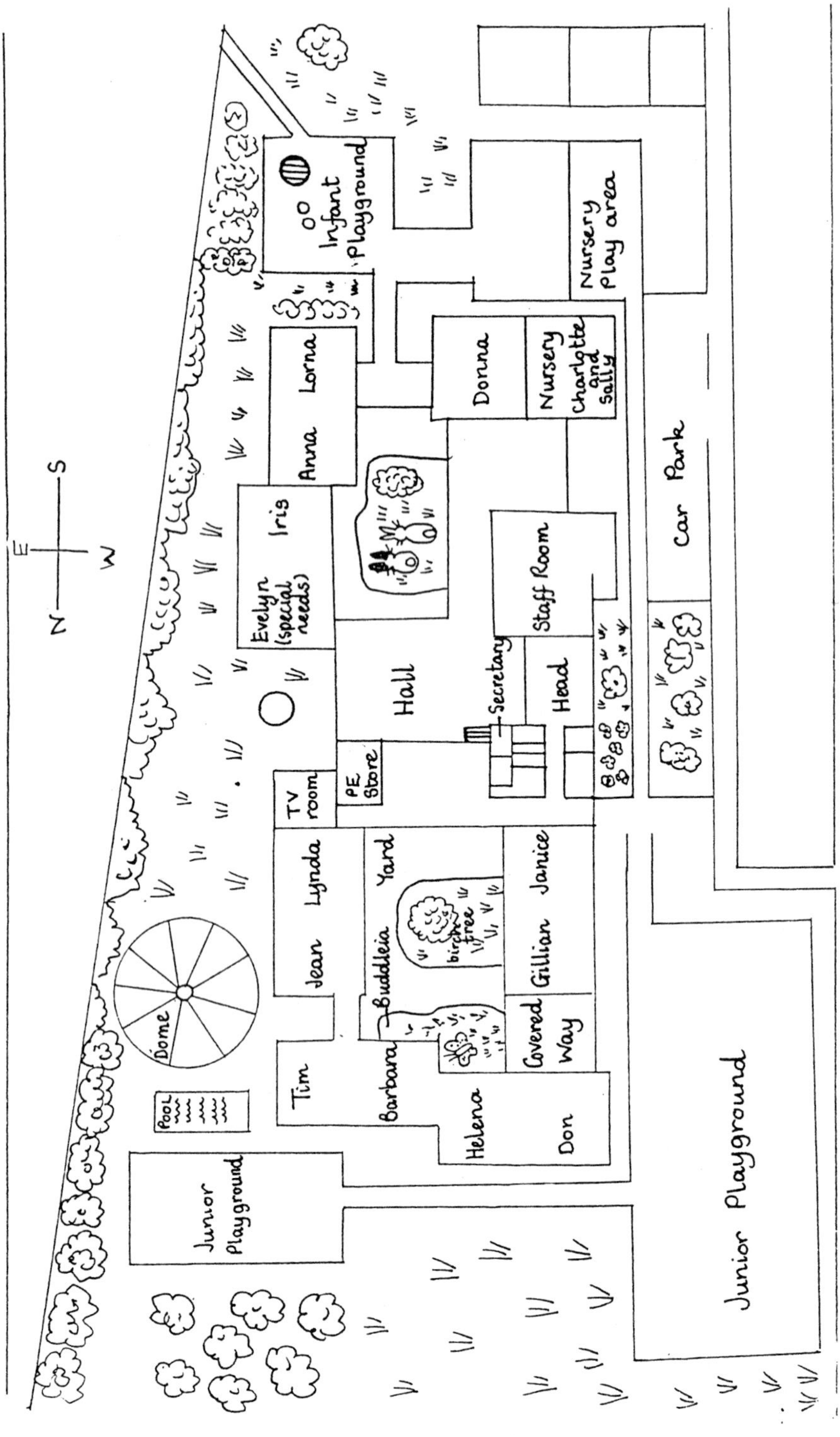

Map 2: Cowper School (September–December)

(Drawn by Lorraine Rainbow)

Chapter 5

Turning the World Upside Down
(September, October)

> Grant that this day we fall into no sin, neither run into
> any kind of danger . . . (Book of Common Prayer)

> O Lord, all the world belongs to you
> And you are always making all things new . . .
> (hymn, Patrick Appleyard)

> God within us all
> Of laughter and of tears
> Prevent us all from walking into danger . . .
> (hymn)

The front page of the local paper had three stories on Friday 19 August. I'd been prepared for the main one by Janice, who was now acting deputy head:

Justin, 7, loses fight for life
BRAVE BOY CHEERFUL TO THE END

Justin was dead, and my first thought was I'd missed his funeral. Then I thought of his mother, who kept on hoping ('the doctors can't believe how well he's doing') just as we are supposed to do. Then — how is Ben? — who was lost the last time I saw him, between all the attention being paid to his tragic older brother, and his new sister. I'd only met Justin's father once.

Janice, Sue and David the caretaker went to the funeral, while I was away on holiday. Justin had chosen the hymns from those he'd learnt at school. One begins:

> O Lord, all the world belongs to you
> And you are always making all things new.
> What is wrong you forgive
> And the new life you live
> Is what's turning the world upside down.

Later, Justin's mother was to tell me that she couldn't remember what hymns they'd sung. Then she read an early draft of this section and asked me to tippex out 'unhappy' from the quotation from his record card: 'Justin was never unhappy . . . I never remember him like that.' And, to tell the truth, neither do I.

Janice and Sue told me:

> The vicar said during the service that Justin was a credit to everyone, including his school . . . the school should be congratulated for the enthusiasm Justin showed for the hymns . . . I know this is odd [said Sue] but although it was terribly sad, it was the nicest funeral you could imagine . . . Quite a few of the mums were there, crying . . . It was awful, what can you say?

According to the paper, Justin's mother had told their reporter: 'He hadn't got a middle name, so he called himself Justin Benjamin Charles Michael Leonard Faye Andrews after his brother, his two grandfathers and even his baby sister.'

In the first assembly of the new term, I told the children that 'our friend Justin Andrews, who'd been in Mrs Marx's class, had died.' Then we sang 'O Lord, all the world', 'once more, for Justin'. The singing was very good for the first day of term. Much later I came across his record card:

> Missed a lot of school through illness . . . a beautiful handwriter . . . he knows initial sounds and can construct his own sentences . . . a bright boy who knows his numbers well, but who misses a lot of practical work through illness . . . very good at art . . .
> July 87 operation on malignant tumour.
> August 88 deceased.

There is a piece of his writing in the file. I'm looking at it now, as I draft this. It's inconsequential, but it was worth a smiley face when it was done, two years ago:

> What is it?
> It feels rough at the bottom
> and on the handle it is smooth
> and the bit that holds the
> rough bit is smooth and round
> It is a potato masher

National politics have flown in from the outside limbo they seemed to inhabit when I was a young man. Certainly, I noticed what governments did until 1978, but only as newspaper stories, sometimes frightening (the Cuba crisis), sometimes encouraging (the general liberalization of human laws in the 1960s). Now, though, they affect every move I make: in my work, in my house, as I move about the city. Soon they will affect me as I stand with Dawn and Daniel on the terraces at the City ground, with our ID cards in our pockets.

Now, in the autumn term of 1988, I'm watching the managers of the caretaking service scurry around to try to meet the Government's demands about privatization. Jimmy Randle's voice is exhausted when I speak to him on the phone about our cleaning problems, and eventually his clerk tells me he is not available 'for the next two weeks while the privatization is sorted out'.

This is an example of an ideological belief — the centrality of competition — having a direct effect on the lives of our children. Many of our schools have not been cleaned all summer, as staff have left to go to more secure, better paid jobs. David the caretaker has been drafted into the management team to try to get these schools up to scratch. He is running around the area, spending an hour at this school, an hour at that . . . His wife is acting caretaker until we make a new appointment.

One of the caretakers said to me six months ago:

It's all deliberate, you know . . . the way the cleaning service is being buggered up — schools'll be dirty soon, and all the middle-class parents will send their kids to private schools and our schools will be left for the working class, the Asians . . .

. . . And what is happening to cleaning [added another county council employee] is going to happen to caretaking and groundstaff, and then eventually to the teaching: death by starvation through a cynical commitment to competition above justice, love, decency . . . we are fighting for our schools — and if we lose the fight, we will be in the dark . . . and being the soggy liberals we are, we will forgive, but we will never forget . . .

How could we ? Because all this comes from a government never out of our minds for one moment. It claims to be anti-ideology, but has brought its ideology into everything.

Another national decision to affect us is the sudden change in the timetable for the election of parent-governors. I rush my letters out, asking for nominations, as within a month we have to meet to co-opt new governors who should have some connection with 'the local business community'. It isn't made clear whether these connections can be through a trade union.

I doubt whether either the longstanding governors or the new co-optees realize how much work they are going to be responsible for, overseeing curriculum and financial management. The world is being turned upside down, and no one is being given a moment to reflect on how to walk on his hands.

And here are the beginnings of the National Curriculum: two A4 books, well designed, but constructed entirely in targets, as though a child only exists in terms of what she might become, not as she is now. They have been chucked our way by Duncan Graham, once a CEO, now Chief Executive and Chairman of the National Curriculum Council. Aside from the targeting framework, the contents seem sound enough. It's no bad thing if they increase the sheer quantity of science taught in primary schools. There has never been enough, though much work has been scientific in character, and simply not recognized as such.

I give both the books to Barbara, who's in charge of keeping us informed on all the NCC does. I tell her that it's being said, though, that the NC will be insignificant in changing schools: what will really bring about the new order will be local management.

As ever, there is not enough time for consultation.

'How did you get on?'
'Well, I got it.'
'Oh. Congratulations . . .'

Sue, over the past five years, has changed from being a polite front-of-house clerk, to being a secretary, dealing with all computer printouts, financial statements, bills; while still being the first point of contact with parents. Now she has a job at the local high school, because she needs a better salary.

I got back from taking a concussed boy to the hospital with his mother ('Try to keep him awake, Mrs Coton') to find a letter, delivered by the violin teacher, telling me that from now on violin tuition will take place between 3.00 and 4.00 on a Friday afternoon.

Dear Mr Sainsbury,
Thank you for the new music timetable.
Could I point out that (a) our school — possibly uniquely among primaries in the area — has its Friday assembly last thing, and all the children and staff attend. And (b) we finish at 3.35 anyway?
Could you therefore re-consider the timing of our violin tuition?
Yours sincerely

The advertisement for Sue's job wasn't placed for three weeks. This meant we had to find a temp, and Sue worked at training Shirley, a parent, in the basic skills: dinner money, capitation, book-keeping, monthly and weekly returns, understanding some of the printouts. I would have to do most of the typing, and I talked to Shirley about confidentiality, answering the phone, etc.

Shirley turns out to be quick at picking up things, good with people . . . but she can't spell. 'What would you do about the typing if you got the job?'
'I'd learn . . .'

Telecom put in a new phone system. It caused four days disruption, relieved, for me anyway, by the technician's interest in jazz. A pianist, he liked the music we were playing in assembly, Bessie Smith singing 'Kitchen Man', with Clarence Williams and Eddie Lang; and the record Barbara was using for dance: 'Elite Syncopations'. Cockney, chuffed to be asked, embarrassed, he turned down Lynda's invitation to play in assembly.

When it was finished, at four o'clock on a Friday afternoon, I buzzed the nursery and breathed at Charlotte.

The music adviser called, and gave us a new violin tuition timetable: the one we wanted. Given the age we live in, this was a little victory of some significance, and consequently we rejoiced.

A story came from Jeanette, now supply teaching in Manchester, through Charlotte. In the staffroom of a school where she was doing supply cover, she put her hand into her bag for her packed lunch and set off her anti-rape screech alarm. 'What was that?' 'My cheese roll.'

The year this book covers is also the year of the re-awakening of my affection for league football. Seven-year-old Daniel has a passion for City that equals mine for Crystal Palace when I was 13. The big difference is that, thirty years ago, I looked up to those mature men on the field, while now I gaze affectionately, patronizingly, censoriously, enviously on young men and boys. I teach Daniel about the game, and see his understanding grow. I wish my understanding of the teaching of poetry would grow as fast, or Simon's of reading, or Margaret's of what our educational psychologist calls 'social skills'.

One result of this is that metaphors from football have sprung to mind as I've written this account of Cowper's year: I've seen myself more as the goalkeeper than as the manager. My friend Mary Jane says that the use of this field of reference is sexist, because I'm excluding more than half the constituency for the book; and that half is predominantly women. But I'd be excluding far more people were my metaphors to come from, say, literary criticism, or synchronized swimming; or from the novels and other assorted prose of Vladimir Nabokov.

Football has figured largely in staffroom conversations I've known, and by no means only among men. Some heads who rarely meet recognize each other's teams on Saturday afternoons: Preston North End, for example, who've 'had a bad decade'; or Derby County, which is my friend's team. Dennis has been a headteacher in another authority for twenty years. He was asked recently to go on a course on 'Stress and the Headteacher'. Are you going? I asked him.

Am I hell! I feel more bloody stress, I told them, at 25 to 5 on a Saturday afternoon when Derby are losing 1-0! . . . The other week I was listening to Radio Derby's commentary on the Millwall-Derby game, I could just about get it [in Tring], it's crackly, but I just about get it, but only on the car radio, and while I was clearing out the car the commentator said, 'We're having a competition to see who's the listener who's furthest away' and I ran indoors and I phoned them up . . . and they kept saying, 'It's still Mr Reilly in Tring' until five minutes from time when they said, 'I've bad news for our listener in Tring' and they'd got a call from Scarborough . . .

Dennis once had a poem published in his club's programme. It was called 'A Debt to Derby County'. He said, in the conversation quoted above:

How can you feel stress at school? . . . you do the best you can, how can you feel stress about things you can't do anything about, like politicians and their ignorance about schools . . .? The local MP came here, and he hadn't a bloody clue about these kids and their schools . . . He thought, if a teacher was away, you just rang the office and they sent another one . . . He'd no idea about the three day rule . . .

Perhaps that reference is exclusive to many readers: it is the rule that states a teacher has to be away for three whole days before you are automatically given supply cover. It will be extinct soon, as Local Management takes over.

Watford came to City, and lost 3-2. The excitement reminded me of Oscar Wilde on smoking a cigarete: the perfect pleasure — exquisite, and it leaves one unsatisfied. There was certainly something exquisite about the cheering as we left the ground, but as satisfaction goes, I wouldn't want to depend on it. When it comes to stress, if I have to suffer it, I'd rather it was about something that mattered.

Charlotte set up an evening for parents. I'd covered Tim's class briefly while he'd hung around the nursery with a camera. As the slides went up, I noticed that Barbara, Janice, Miriam (the deputy designate) and I — the non-nursery staff who were present — were all sitting on one side of the room; and that the parents and Sally — the nursery nurse — were on the other. Charlotte was in the middle, working the slide projector.

She talked about the importance of play in learning, implying strongly that sand and water, for example, might be used for teaching various concepts higher up the school. Only one parent voiced serious disagreement with this, mentioning secondary schools and qualifications. But Charlotte and I felt that she spoke for other parents who (to quote one of them afterwards) were 'afraid to ask questions in case I look stupid'. Two of the teachers, who'd had children in secondary schools, pointed out that GCSE required a more practical approach, for which nursery work provided an excellent grounding.

Janice, as acting deputy, had collected from the rest of the staff examples of learning through play. She began listing them: '. . . and then Mr Snaid, who has the oldest children, told me about a game he plays with the children using

Illustrations 4-7: The children's work after the African exhibition

Illustration 4

dice. They roll the dice and see what numbers come up most when the two dice are added together . . . they are learning about probability . . .'

They are also doing sums, I wanted to shout — in my impatience to get at the fact that schools have not changed that much. You still learn to add up, and subtract; to read and to write. Schools have not changed as much as some people think they have; not as much as they should have.

My second headship, for example, between 1981 and 1984, was in a school, that, like many an educational publisher, had not had the 1960s. There was still surreptitious smacking, open sarcasm and general intimidation. There was no notion of the value of work done around objects, like stones, or scientific

Illustration 5

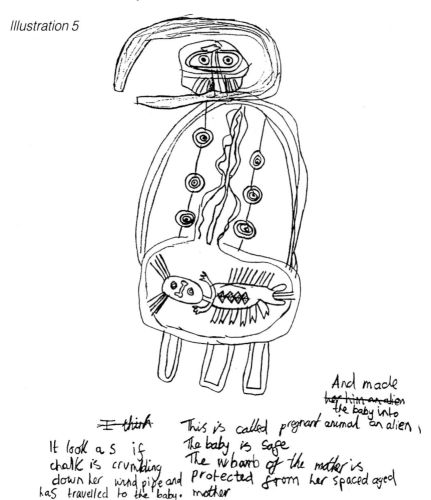

And made ~~her him an alien~~
the baby into

~~I think~~ This is called pregnant animal an alien,

It look as if   The baby is safe
chalk is crumbling   The w barb of the mother is
down her wind pipe and protected from her spaced aged
has travelled to the baby.   mother

experiments, or stuffed animals. There was no evidence of the influence of books like Clegg's *The Excitement of Writing,* or Margaret Langdon's *Let the Children Write.* The Plowden Report need not have been commissioned, let alone written.

This is Friday afternoon assembly in my first term at Brampton Church Primary. After the children have read, sung, acted, etc., I say, 'Mrs Jackson [deputy head] could you tell us about the houses please?'

Well, Mr Sedgwick, the yellows have achieved — 289 points [groans from all yellows, slight intakes of breath from blues, reds and greens] and the greens [more, but different, groans] have attained 354 [intensified green groans, breathing from reds and blues hardened]. The blues [groans and barely hidden aspirated cheers] have attained

409 points and . . . [mutterings, and more or less what, under different circumstances, would be behaviour for the subtraction of points] the reds 546 [intensified aspirated cheers] . . .

I told the staff early on how I'd like to be rid of this, but the junior teachers (6) voted against me and the infant teachers (4) for me. I eventually got rid of house points, at least partly through the Greek currency method: 'Oh, that's a nice drawing, Damien. 7000 housepoints . . .'

This always goes through my mind when people talk about the radical 1960s. I could show them many places where they never played Joni Mitchell LPs, read Lady Chatterley, grew their hair long or wore kaftans. And I think using words like 'sums', if it reassures parents, is no bad thing. We all want to be linked to our comforting past at times.

. . . Back to Cowper in 1988: although Janice had fourteen examples of learning through play, a conversation with the parents did emerge. Despite some anxiety about the 'play way', there was also a concern that the children should be as happy in the main school as they had been in the nursery.

Then the parents were invited to play with sand, the computer, paint, crayons, water — and many of the parents accepted. The paintings were stereotypical and dull, without movement; anxious to be correct rather than inventive. Sally put them up in the entrance hall.

After the meeting Charlotte said to me: 'I think it was OK . . . I'd have liked more informality, though, there wasn't enough criticism . . . Somebody got started, and then her point got lost. I don't mind people disagreeing, I think it ought to be brought out into the open . . .' Sally said: 'I'd prepare them more another time . . . I'd get them to think of questions they'd like to ask before they came . . .' Miriam said it was 'lovely'. As she got into her car afterwards, we planned the next session between us. 'It's a great school, but there's plenty to do, isn't there?' 'Oh yes', I said. 'It would be a bit dull for you if there wasn't!' I slammed the car door. Damn cheek! What does she mean, it's not perfect?

'Interviews are like childbirth — hell to go through, but you're filled with weariness and elation afterwards.' This was Miriam talking about the interview day. The candidates, two men and three women, had arrived for coffee at 10.30, and both the adviser (who wasn't to stay for the interviews) and I showed them round. In each classroom, the candidates got down to the children, looking at their work, commenting on displays to each other, to the class teacher, and to me.

The adviser whispered, 'All this lot will make a good deputy head, but you've got to find a round peg for a round hole . . .' One of them, a singer and guitarist, was pleased to be commandeered for a music lesson with infants. The rest looked slightly uncomfortable for a moment, as if wrong-footed by this lucky chance to display a talent valuable in any primary school.

In the interviews, I always began with what I thought was an easy question, about the candidate's specialism: 'What is the function of music in a primary school? . . . How do you go about teaching children to write? . . . Where are special needs going next? . . . What does a classroom look like where there is lots of good science going on?'

One candidate commented how the panel were all men. 'Yes, but the candidates aren't', I said. Then, when I asked, 'How long will you stay if you're appointed?' she replied, 'Oh, come on! The stock question! Am I interested in headship?' Nettled, I replied, 'Just answer it for now, and I'll go back to textbooks on interviewing techniques later . . .' 'Well, yes, I suppose I am . . .' The officer asked questions about national developments: 'Do you think the new curriculum will change schools like this?' 'I certainly hope not!' 'Yes, that's what many of us hope, but what do you predict?'

Miriam came from a local church school, and has a contrasting background in inner London. She has a well-known commitment to the discarding of reading schemes, in favour of mainstream books. She smoked nervously all day, and then said after the appointment that she wouldn't be smoking in school. This is probably just as well, because Sue was our last smoker.

Miriam was overjoyed to be offered the job. 'I thought it would be Terry' (the singer). I looked forward with excitement to working closely with someone who thinks and feels about children and their learning the same as I do, in almost every respect. What a ghastly responsibility it is! What a sad phenomenon is the head realizing over a period of a year or so that he and the governors have got it wrong, and appointed a deputy head who's unsympathetic to the way the school is going.

Mr Sedgwick smacks people when they are naughty.

He makes them do maths when they are naughty.

Mr Sedgwick is nice when you are good. He has whiskers as well.

Headmasters write a lot. When you are naughty he goes mad and crazy.

Mr Sedgwick works a lot and has a whip.

Mr Sedgwick has a beard.

Mr Sedgwick likes sitting in assembly and reading a story.

— Lorna's 5-year-old infants.

I'm sorry about this, but:
all the toilets were vile yesterday following unpleasant things being

done in them. I will speak to the children about it, but could you say to them that

1) they should treat them with respect

2) that if I catch anyone mucking about — and I'm going to be checking — I'll make the child and his/her parents clean it up

3) that if they feel ill they should tell us.

Could you, for a while, make sure that only one child from your class is in the loo at the same time.

Sorry. Thanks.

Despite this hastily phrased note, the problems persisted. We appointed two fourth-year juniors to check the toilets, but there was still a mess in one. Eventually I isolated one boy who was seen going to the loo without permission. The loo was later flooded.

NOTE TO STUDENTS OF BONSALL CAMPUS
This shows me a poor light: but how else do you deal with this problem?

'Ian, did you go to that toilet?'
'No.'
'But Mr S————— saw you.'
'I did, but I asked Miss H—————.'
[not true]
I assume that Ian is the cuprit, and I find the classroom ancillary who helps him clean the toilet. She then cleans his hands with Dettol.

The problem ceases. His mother complains: 'To make a child do that!' I am not proud of my part in this, though pragmatically pleased the problem is over.

Lynda came back from another interview in Shrewsbury:

It's such a long way to go for another failure! I was up at half past four this morning! They appointed two probationers . . . one of them was a tall, dark trendy gent rather like Nick Haymen from the Levi Stone Wash advert. He was obviously on to a winnner. He was doing ceramics at secondary — but being the token man, and good looking, was impressive. Perhaps he had toyboy status for the head and the deputy, both middle-aged ladies like me! . . . He was a nice bloke, would have gone down well at Cowper . . .

I don't think they were interested in someone my age . . . I showed them those computer pictures, and they said, ooh, that's nice, colour, that's posh, they hadn't got anything like that . . . They said, these articles you write for *Art and Craft,* that must be a nice little sideline for you. They weren't impressed. I think they wanted someone they could manipulate, I was too experienced for them.

Illustration 6

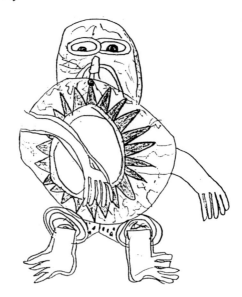

This drawing is done by batik. It is only a bit of the Picture. It looks like he is holding the Sun.

The other successful candidate was in a private school, and she'd done a lot of work about Egypt as part of a topic and they asked what was the practical application of that and she told them they'd taken the children to Egypt as part of the topic, and that shut them up.

Like Lynda, I'm always pleased to see any panel silenced (unless it's one I'm on), but I was even more impressed here by that evidence of the gap between what different children get, depending on what their parents earn.

In the third week of September, there is a relaxed feeling among the staff. We are going through a spell of glorious red-brown weather, with the sun brighter than a pound coin. Somebody says at least the Government has no control over that — or will they privatize it? says someone else. Like they will the roads: tracts of sunshine will be bought up by those not wishing to mingle with the rest of us. You'll be on a school trip, and you'll find somewhere to eat your sandwiches, when — What do you think you are doing, enjoying autumn sunshine here? This is private sunshine. Clear off.

The light shines through the big windows on to fresh work: paintings about the harvest, of course, and writing about contrasts, the agreed theme for the half-term, with black and white op-art designs and other art ideas in prominence. The staff have chosen two contrasting records each for assemblies, so we get: the 1812 overture and John Lennon's 'Imagine'; Gershwin's

Illustration 7

it looks like an eye with a thousand eyes inside it.

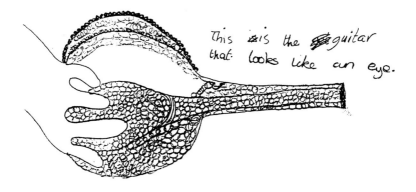

This is the guitar that looks like an eye.

'Summertime', in the Janis Joplin version, and 'Summer' from 'The Four Seasons'; Stephane Grappelli and a romantic violin concerto; Kathleen Ferrier singing 'O Waly Waly' and Bessie Smith singing 'You Got to Give Me Some' and 'Kitchen Man'; Acker Bilk playing 'Stranger on the Shore', and the slow movement of the Mozart concerto.

In the third week of September, the children walk around calmly, not hyped up for Christmas yet; not controlled by any gusty bad weather; happy, working, beginning things. The staff face the near-wholeness of the year cheerfully.

During the summer holidays a publisher had asked me for two song lyrics for a new book of assembly material, and in the fourth week of September, we sang one of them at Cowper.

> The tunes are traditional — good ones, after all they've lasted, and they're free, because they're out of copyright . . . but we're commissioning the words from writers . . . The best ones will probably come from poets, but who've also done a few assemblies in their time!

Being called a poet, with an offer of £40 for a song, was irresistible. What would Lynda and the children make of 'Song for a Rainy Morning'?

We've run through the rain
That's pushing at the door.
It's dripping from the oak and lime,
The shiny sycamore.
God within us all
Of meadow, lake and shore,
Prevent us all from running into danger.

We've walked to the hall.
Our friends are standing near.
If rain or clouds should rule today
Or if the sky should clear
God within us all
Of laughter and of tears
Prevent us all from walking into danger.

The tune is one that traditionally goes to the words that define jingoism: 'We don't want to fight/But by jingo if we do/We've got the guns, we've got the men/we've got the money too . . .'

The new song suited the rainy weather that turned up in October. The other song was 'Song for a Sunny Morning':

Here we stand
This sunny morning
Light pours down
On cheerful songs.
May our words
Be like sun on water
For us all
As day grows long.

In the town
This sunny morning
People walk
From door to door.
News is spread
Through glittering airwaves,
Peaceful news
And news of war.

As the hands
Move round the clockface
And our work
Gets underway
Here we stand
For peace in our corner
Of this world

This sunny day.
(from *Wake Up Stir About,* Unwin Hyman)

This tune is called East Virginia. Are my words political? I wonder now — after all, they do mention peace.

'It doesn't seem much fun.' 'Did he go into the right profession?' 'What about some celebration?' 'What about the wit and urbanity Cowper's famous for?' 'Have you conveyed the feeling that something's happened that you've initiated?' These are some real and imagined objections to all the foregoing; and it may be true that how much I enjoy my job hasn't come through either the appalled recognition of what the Philistines have in mind for our future, or the scraps of day-to-day existence that take over my energies and this account.

Well, here are two things I celebrated in October 1988:

Six Ways of Looking at an Eye

Red ivy crawling up a white wall,
a black spot in the middle of nowhere.
It's an oval shape like an egg you get for Easter
or a spy looking for dangerous crimes.
Black spider's legs on an end of a leaf.
It's a curl wrapped around nothing.

(Pauline, 9)

'Six Ways of Looking' is a writing idea from Sandy Brownjohn's book, *Does It Have to Rhyme?* (Hodder and Stoughton). She in turn derived it from Wallace Stevens' poem, 'Thirteen Ways of Looking at a Blackbird'. It all depends on your convincing the children that there are more ways of looking at something than the one you first thought of — and it's usually easier to do this with children than it is with adults. Here's Danielle's 'Six Ways of Looking at a Torch', from the same session:

It's a bandit running on the streets, loose.
It's a spy out and about,
looking for a robber.
It's a maze of streets
— I know he's there somewhere! —
It's a robot
when he's spotted his enemy.

It's a sense of ice
cold upon the world, ripples on the water
splashing on the rocks,
a sad face with tears running down,
a pool of blood, the shimmer in it.

111

It's a pair of eyes,
blue, green, yellow,
a hollow tree
just waiting
to be chopped down,
a sound fading away
in the distance.

It's a spotlight
hitting the star of our show,
a mass of colours in a whirl
to make a gold colour,
or the sun with its hypersonic beam.
It's a disco as the lights
flicker on and off,
a silver ring repeated again in the night,
a golden morning that can't wait to begin.

It's a collage just finished,
a help gadget always ready to help
unless the batteries run down.
It's a Spanish doll
dancing.

Danielle's original had been:

a spot light looking at the star of our show.
a sense of ice cold apon the world.
the ripples in the water splashing on the rocks.
the sun with its hipasonik beam.
a spy on the loose looking for a rober.
a pool of blood, the shimmer in it.
a golden morning that cant wait to begin
a robot when hes spotted his enamy the light sudden flash's on
a bandit running on the streets loose
a mass of coulors in a worl to make a gold coulor
a silver ring lost repeat again in the light
a horror moon shown up on everyone
a holiday sun not in England this year
a mase of streets I know he's there somewhere
a dico as the lights flicker on and of
a help gaget all way's ready to help unles the batary's have run down
a colage just finished
a sad face with tear's running down
a sound fading away in the distance
a pair of eyes blue green yellow
a spainish doll danceing

Danielle had written that first draft for me in about twenty minutes. I had corrected the spelling and some of the punctuation, and let her get on with her maths. But that evening I looked again at her work: untidy, incorrect, splashy, uncontrolled, it was its own stuff, an original piece that stemmed from thinking about a gift, a torch. So the next morning at 8.30, I said, in the presence of her mother, Charlotte, that I'd typed her writing up, and that she might like to re-draft it with scissors and paste into an order that brought together similar themes. Her face looked sceptical, but she agreed. An hour later I found her in Helena's room preparing the version that begins 'It's a bandit . . .'

The pleasure for me is a fresh view of the power of drafting, though I don't think that in every respect the redrafted version is superior. But the learning about words, and her own relationship with them, that I can infer from this material, encourages me to think that some education goes on that targets and objectives won't comprehend.

The other cause for celebration in October was a visit made to the Burns Elliott Hall by Helena with her class and me to see an exhibition of Yoruba art. I made notes about this at the time, and these are extracts from them:

> . . . Because the children had already seen a Yoruba artist close-up, they were ready to enjoy the work at the gallery; they were ready not to find it, as Emmanuel had said, 'primitive' or 'quaint' . . . We asked the children to take five minutes to look at everything in the room, and in that time choose one thing that interested them. 'We want you to take one thing in that picture, and study it — draw it, maybe, or write notes about it, or both. Examine it minutely, carefully, use your pencils in as many different ways as you can . . .'

I was pleased that a passing member of Her Majesty's Inspectorate appreciated the quality of the experience the children were getting: 'I admire the confidence with which your children look at these pictures, and the way they use their pencils . . . their concentration is admirable . . . I wish I could find the time to see how you are going to follow this up . . . What are you thinking of doing . . .?'

In my experience, inspectors and advisers who like what your children are doing always try to push it further. This one never saw the follow-up the next morning. I had had no part in it. Helena sent for me towards the end of the morning. The children were waiting with a satisfied excitement on their faces, and various kinds of work in front of them: one girl, for example, had translated her drawing of a hand playing a guitar — which in turn had been a copy of a bead construction — into something that had more in common with the original: a collage of kidney beans, lentils, split peas, and paint. A boy had changed his drawing of a batik original into a wax resist, and Kate had made a chalk and crayon drawing out of pencil sketches, on which she had written, while still in the gallery: 'This is called the pregnant animal. The baby is safe. The womb of the mother is protected from her space-age mother. It looks as if the chalk is crumbling down her windpipe and has travelled to her baby and made the baby into an alien . . .'

This is not wonderful prose, but evidence of Kate's moving towards an idea on which she might base a poem later. It is as near as most of us are privileged to get to witnessing the process of learning, and something similar can be said of the sketches the children made at the gallery. Here is Kate's poem as she wrote it at school:

It looks like the chalk is crumbling
down the windpipe.
The alien looks like an alien type.
The staring eyes inside the mother look
like a bird's eye view of a hovercraft
and the baby's floating like a raft.
A moving monster with three legs
inside the baby looks like a whole load of pegs . . .

I celebrate a kind of provisional intensity, a pleasure children show, with their notes, their sketches and their conversations, working with a difficult text. I celebrate my own part in that pleasure: the fact that I am not a deliverer of a curriculum, but a sharer in the learning.

Tony, from Edinburgh Road, was at the teachers' centre this evening. He said: 'I went to Yorkshire in the summer and I saw a poster advertising an exhibition, and your friend Emmanuel was in it. It said "Jegede has exhibited in London, Kingston Jamaica, Lagos . . . and at Cowper Primary School, ————shire". I thought you'd like to know! . . .'

Four O'Clock Dance

The children leave the building

Alex and Katrina
Adam Unbenham and James
Alison Greengown and Mac

The children leave the building

autumn leaf and leaf and leaf
and smell of burning in the air
and scarlet roses and scarlet roses
and the one silver birch left

and Ford and Citroen and Renault
And Opel and Volvo and old Vauxhall

The children leave the building

There is no dance and no drama
no painting no poem no page of sums
no songs to sing no construction to be constructed
and checked and measured and drawn
or drawn and measured and checked
and constructed

There is no debate no instrumental playing

There is no art no science no religion

The children leave the building

Katrina and Simone and Jeremy and Nathan
and Syreeta and the other Simone and James
and Gareth and Alan and Margaret and Jane
And Simon and Damien and Mark

and I sit and play the piano
and I sit and paint

and yawn

Rose and bulb and rose
and bulb and rose and
bulb

and autumn leaves

Her GP had suggested to Mrs Carroway that 7-year-old Jimmy's behaviour might be, at least in part, due to food colourings. She came to see me:

> He's no better, is he? He's been a little sod at home. I tried all that stuff about the yellow colourings, and it's not made a blind bit of difference, Mr Sedgwick, not a blind bit of difference. He needs firm handling he does, he needs firm handling. He needs more discipline . . .

Another woman, on her very different, but equally disruptive son: 'I don't want him to go to special school — he's a bleeder, Mr Sedgwick, but I love him.'

Jean-Marie's mother, Mrs Smith: 'I know she's good at art, but that's no good, is it? I tell her, scribble, scribble, scribble all you want my dear, but it's not going to get you a job, now is it?'

To the Manager
——————— City FC

Dear Mr ————,
I gather that the first team squad occasionally visits schools for training sessions and to meet the children. You would be very welcome here, where there are many of your supporters.

I look forward to hearing from you.
Yours sincerely

The juniors were singing one of 'my' hymns in assembly this morning ('Here We Stand') and Charlotte came by from the nursery. This was a conversation in the staffroom later:

Charlotte [to Lynda]: That was a nice hymn the children were singing.
Me: Which one?
Lynda: Fred wrote that —
Me: Shush! Come on, Charlotte, which one did you like?
Charlotte [to Lynda]: Which one did he write?
Me: No, which one did you like?
Charlotte: The one about 'people walk from door to door' —
Me: [cry of victory]
Lynda: He wrote that.
Charlotte [incredulously]: You wrote that?
Me: Yup. The words. That hurt, didn't it?
Charlotte: Yes, that certainly did . . .

Another assembly: I hadn't prepared anything, so I grabbed one of my surefire stories off the shelf in my room: Oscar Wilde's 'The Selfish Giant'. This always spellbinds children, of whatever age: especially when the giant stops being selfish, and puts the little boy in the tree. Later, when the giant sees the wounds in the child's hands and feet, the school is silent, wondering (I think) along with the giant, who is this person? Then the story ends '. . . they found the giant lying dead under the tree, all covered with white blossom', and the atmosphere has to be broken quickly, '. . . and now we'll sing "When a Knight Won His Spurs . . .". It's best not to ask questions, but instead to let Wilde's lovely prose do its job alone.

Other things I use as the assembly man: poems about school by Kit Wright, John Walsh and Alan Ahlberg; poems by Charles Causley; poems from my anthology of commissioned pieces (*This Way That Way*) (Mary Glasgow); stories about Little Pete by Leila Berg; Bible stories: the Prodical Son, the Good

Samaritan, David and Goliath, the Creation, Jonah, the Wedding at Cana; stories from a book of world religions. But the best assemblies are made up of children showing each other what they've done: reading, holding up pictures and models, singing, dancing, acting: celebrating their humanity.

As a rule, books made up of prepared assembly material are useless, because they have a tone of voice in them that is entirely the compiler's. How can they work for me? Later in the day, a 4-year-old boy says to Charlotte, as I open the nursery door: 'Here comes the assembly man.'

I thought of the Bonsall Campus when the three students turned up. They all seemed bright, interested people, and we looked forward to a loosening of the staffing constraints for the four weeks while they were here, and to hearing about current thinking about classrooms.

Maggie played the piano in assembly on her first Friday in school. John and Liz also got quickly into the spirit of the place. Each of the three had some time off sick, reminding us of the exhaustion of teaching practice, and how you simply get used to working in the profession.

I asked John what they had to do for preparation:

> We have to get our plans approved by our teacher, then by our supervising tutor, then by the subject tutor for every subject, English, Maths, Science, Social Studies, the lot . . . that's quite a lot of decision-making we've got to get approved before we even start . . .

The tutors varied. One seemed obsessed with record books, as though you could prove your professionalism with the quality of your handwriting, or your rigour with the purchasing and sticking down of reinforcement rings. For this man, the file was everything. He avoided the staffroom, turned down cups of instant, and had a lecture in four parts to respond to any casual comment anyone made. Real life wasn't for him. He preferred subject dividers and preparation.

The other tutors seemed in tune with the nature of the school, ready to laugh at current educational events: the imposition of the National Curriculum, the provision of opting out facilities, open enrolment, Local Financial Management: 'What could be funnier than you lot being accountants?' said one of them. 'And what more do you need to join this profession these days, other than a sense of the bloody ridiculous?' Then later, the same tutor, on a painting by Margaret:

> That is lovely . . . that is what education's about, the time that kid had doing that picture, and what went through her mind and heart as she did it . . . It's nothing to do with objectives, targets, management . . . when there's still that moment . . . you can see the child's understanding grow . . .

Lynda came back from another interview just before half term:

The head gave me a lift to the station afterwards and he said I wasn't positive enough, my aims and objectives weren't clear enough . . . I felt that playing the piano was the be-all and end-all. They said, if it had been an art post, you'd've got it . . . It was a very nice school, lots of lovely pastel drawing, but limited artwise . . . There was only one other candidate, a student, very homely, sensible shoes, and she got it . . . I don't know whether I'm going to get a job, it's very discouraging to keep going over there and to come back empty-handed . . .

Often probationers get the jobs Lynda goes for, I thought. It's because they're cheaper, of course, and when Local Management comes in, we'll all be making decisions for this sort of utterly uneducational reason. Like doctors prescribing drugs, not because they're the right ones, but because they're the ones the practice can afford, interviewing panels will be thinking, not what can she do that we need doing, but, how much will we have to pay her?

The Philistines, who were loud at the door ten years ago, are inside the temple, ripping down learning and replacing it with the idol cost-effectiveness. A local church school opted for Mammon in a disarmingly open way by being sponsored by a bank. Another school persuaded an estate agent to sponsor the assembly accompanist, though I couldn't find out whether, football-wise, the pianist was wearing the words 'MEES HOUSEFINDERS' across her back.

Mrs Andrews came to see me. I held Faye while her mother looked through a draft of this.

1979. The party of 8- and 9-year-olds from Swing Gate First School in Hertfordshire (my first headship) had visited Singleton Open Air Museum, Marwell Park Zoo, Fishbourne Roman Palace and HMS Victory (coming down the gang-plank afterwards: 'Who was this Nelson, anyway?'). They had thrown pine cones at each other in a clearing in the New Forest, and eaten ice creams at the Beaulieu Motoring Museum. They had wilted in the heat at Stonehenge, and drunk coke in the garden of a roadside pub. Now they walked round the cathedral at Chichester.

What struck me at the time was the power of the meeting of, on the one hand, centuries of orthodox Anglican Christianity, and, on the other, centuries of visual art. 'Two beautiful twelfth-century stone carvings . . . depicting Christ on his way to raise Lazarus from the dead and, secondly, the miracle performed . . . Bishop Langdon's great window, of the early fourteenth-century . . . portraits damaged beyond recognition by Cromwellian soldiers . . . John Piper's modern tapestry in vivid colouring, hanging from a sixteenth-century oak screen . . . Graham Sutherland's painting 'Noli me tangere' in the chapel of St Mary Magdalene . . .'

The Shell Guide does not mention the Larkin poem, copied out in elegant italic, at the side of an Arundel tomb. A Victorian had altered the stone-work drastically, to make the earl and countess hold hands, 'to prove', as Larkin says, 'Our almost-instinct almost true: What will survive of us is love'; though there is no evidence that Larkin knew that it was a sentimental Victorian bowdlerization that had led to his marvellous poem. Nor does the guide mention the Chagall window, with its electric colours depicting the animals of God's creation: another crossing here: not only Anglican Christianity and art, but Judaism.

I don't remember what impression this made on the children from Hertfordshire. They would probably have sooner been on the beach, or in the forest. Whatever they or my colleagues were thinking, I decided in the nave of Chichester Cathedral that I'd be a headteacher, somewhere, one day, of a school that collected art.

As you walk through the dining area at Cowper, you pass two prints by the Indian artist, Saleem Arif, who did a residency once at the Burns Elliot Hall. They are airy designs of horses, and human hands and feet. We bought these with the help of subsidies from the art adviser. There is also a framed press photograph of four of our children working with him. In contrast, there are two prints by Emmanuel: one we bought with school funds, and another he gave us. The first is a boldly-made face, half covered with the figure's hands, the second a more complicated design of mysterious figures intermingling.

There is a five-foot square acrylic a young painter left us after he'd spent a week in the nursery, while applying for a place at art school: red, blue, purple; jagged bright lines and shapes above the fiction library. We paid £50 for that with a gift from the football club that hires our field and dome for training. There are two more prints in the top library, bought again with the help of funds supplied by the art adviser: a half-abstract, half-representational egg design in red, yellow and orange; and a strange black and white thing in geometric shapes. Lynda and Lorna chose these at an exhibition.

There are pictures teachers leaving have given us: a pencil drawing of a sunflower head that I often use as an example of looking closely. The last nursery teacher gave us that. There is a set of four pastel drawings of hedgerow flowers that Jan worked on herself, before she left, two years ago. There is also a picture a friend gave me in 1968 that stays most of the time at Cowper.

Then there is the art loan scheme. Once we had a set of large abstract sculptures for a term, but mostly this work is in reproduction: right now a Picasso blue period, but with the colour gone watery; a Klee cat; an Andrew Wyeth of a sickly looking girl in bed, looking out through open windows, with white curtains flying; a familiar Gauguin, with the colour (again) diluted; a Canalletto; and some Indian pictures of palaces and princesses.

Teachers bring in art too: African heads, and sketches of birds done by a friend, and handed over, Gully Jimson-like, for the price of a pint and a packet of cigarettes, years and years ago; and paintings and drawings from a remarkable collection that belongs to Jackie, the part-time teacher, and her husband. These pictures don't stay on the walls of the dining room or the library. Teachers take them to classrooms, and children imitate and copy them, talk and write about them; or just look at them. In Iris's room in October, a group are looking at a Chagall cut-out, and working with bright paper and scissors. In the nursery, the children are studying buildings, so they have the Canalletto in there, and an Indian palace, alongside the building bricks they've cadged from somewhere, and a trowel and a cement-mixer. The children have made models, collages and paintings of walls and houses, and these are displayed around the room as if they mattered. Which they do.

Art opens up the possibility of freedom. Otherwise people would not suppress it, starve it, throw stones at it. I'm glad it's all over the place at Cowper.

There's a visitor in the nursery. He's had enough, he tells us, of supply teaching in secondary schools, and wants to become a nursery teacher. He's spent a week with us, and right now he's talking with a group of children about teddy bears.

Charlotte is calming Anthony down: his heart is going like mad, and apparently he cannot help but run yelling round the room when he arrives. Once he hit Charlotte in the face. Michael (Miranda's brother — she had the convulsion in March) is similar. His insistence on all their attention is almost painful for teachers at times, as is his utter lack (or so it seems — can it be so?) of a sense of humour. Twice in three weeks he has clambered on a pipe in the lavatory, and snapped it under the cistern. His father says to me:

> You know what his problem is, don't you? Don't you? He's hyperactive, same as his sister . . . He can't be left, not for a moment, nor can his sister . . . They've ruined my life between them, ruined my life, and their mother's . . . I'm sending him to bed as soon as he gets home and he's missing his treat he's been so much looking forward to . . . He'll get out of bed for his meal, and then it's straight back in . . .

Charlotte is saying, as Anthony struggles, 'We don't get enough information about special needs children when they come . . . Sometimes I feel we're just left to get on with it . . .'

Three girls are concentrating on a combined collage, with a quietness that contrasts with these two boys. Two other boys are sitting on little armchairs, reading books from the book tray. A group of parents have accepted cups of coffee from Sally, and, as they drink them, they watch children beginning paintings of human figures. Lorraine, the trainee nursery nurse, is writing in a reporter's notebook for her college study. Ben is kissing his mother goodbye for the afternoon. Mrs Andrews will push the pram home, and get on with more life without Justin. I will find Bryan, a governor, and ask him to make a tape for Justin's grandmother, of children singing.

Chapter 6

Special Needs (November, December)

Christmas! Puttin' the trimmins' up! Their favourite time. (Gwen Dunn, *Simon's Last Year* Methuen)

What a pair of miseries (*The Sun,* 1987)

Prodnose: One never knows when you are being serious.
Myself: Apparently one doesn't, you great bat-eared gawk!
(Beachcomber (J.B. Morton), *By the Way*)

He hath put down the mighty from their seats, and exalted them of low degree. (Luke 1:52)

Who is at their best as winter spreads over longer and longer parts of the day? Nearly everybody at school has a cold, and Anna, the long-term supply teacher who is covering till Miriam arrives, is off for a week as both her children have been ill, consecutively rather than concurrently. When she rings us she sounds terrible, her folk singer's contralto reduced to a croak. 'Now I've got this fluey thing . . . perhaps moving house and taking on full-time at once was a bit much . . . I hope to be back on Monday, I'll give you a ring Sunday night if I'm not going to get in . . .' It is difficult for anyone who is running a home and teaching full-time, but the immediate problem for school is coping with the absences: first, getting supply cleared, and then, once a compromise between getting cover and muddling through is negotiated, finding a teacher. Sometimes this class get an excellent teacher called Chris, but she is moving and getting married. Sometimes they have me, and sometimes they are split between the other infant classes.

This is fair on neither the children nor the teachers, but who cares about such details now? I met a man at a party who talked like a *Daily Mail* editorial, and who represents the dominant views on these matters: opinions from which the teaching profession is normally protected. Too often, we assume that our genial humanism is a dogma respected in the saloon bar, in the office, in the estate agent's, on the terraces. A meeting with Mr *Daily Mail,* who doesn't have to worry about interest rates and unemployment, is an informative experience every now and then:

> I'm all for this opting out business and it doesn't matter that the school can't opt in again if a different set of parents have different views, the parents will simply sell the school down the swannee if it's no good . . . I'll be frank with you, I'm anti-teacher, there's no one harder to please than me as far as schools are concerned. . . Standards are dropping, look at the way teachers dress nowadays . . . Schools should junk multicultural education and get back to the basic skills, that's what parents are telling them to do . . . Schools ought to stop whingeing about not having spare teachers when someone's away, how do you think industry manages? . . .

He was dressed in an immaculate blazer with silver buttons, grey flannels, and a navy, scarlet and white striped tie. His hair was parted straight as a touchline. Drinking Perrier (I was driving that evening), and dressed in jeans and my favourite shirt — a heavy, navy blue, cold weather affair that would have looked as good on the rugby field as it did at this party — I demurred.

Driving home in the dark midnight of mid-December, we thought of our adventure next Easter: a holiday in Egypt, made possible by Dawn's supply teaching, and an increase in my freelance earnings: in particular a comic piece in *The Guardian* about my Aunt, and some articles about education in *The Times Educational Supplement* and *The Guardian* that had caused some offence. We talked about publishing and how some things touched a nerve, and others didn't, as we drove through the night. Egypt seemed a long way off.

November. The curtains were drawn across the windows in the assembly hall at Henry Grigson Comprehensive. Following a three-line whip, all the primary heads were gathered on plastic chairs in congregational rows to listen to those officers who were most informed about the National Curriculum: the new high priests of education, who had roughly displaced both charismatic Chief Education Officers like Alec Clegg, Tim Brighouse and John Newsom; and any number of advisers, who had won their spurs and any respect they valued by being professional in the schools, with the children: in the thick of the good fight.

Whatever light the winter day had to offer was denied us from 1.30 pm on. I sat at the back with friends, overhearing the occasional unfair ribald joke at the expense of the administrators of our authority; noting the style of one of them: Eastwood shrug, hooded eyes, repeating his every last phrase: 'We'd better accept the matter, the National Curriculum is here to stay. Here to stay.' He did a slow dance in his smart dark suit behind the table, his face frequently contorted into a smile. He is a handsome man, and I was impressed by his total commitment to please, his cool drawl. Looking at him, I almost regretted discovering *The Guardian* and draft bitter when I was 18: perhaps I could have been like this . . . urbane, fit . . .?

We looked forward to a break, but the milk turned out to be UHT: like the National Curriculum documents, preserved by force of unnatural pressure. There were scotch eggs, little triangular sandwiches, vol-au-vents, sausages on sticks. Jerry said: 'They should be spending the money on my school's capitation, not this nonsense . . .' Afterwards, in small groups, some of us deplored the fact that there were no women listed in the team of contributors who wrote the paper on school development plans: 'Wouldn't it have been more, at least, well, tactful, to have had some women on a panel that will affect a section of the profession that is overwhelmingly female . . .?' 'I think we should get down to some serious issues . . . this is a sideline as far as this document is concerned . . . Let's be grateful that someone is trying to help us in these difficult times . . .', said someone.

In fact, in November, no further news had come from the National Curriculum Council since the maths and science target systems had been published. As the darkness deepened (Oh Lord with me abide) we wondered in the back row what would happen to the arts: dance, art, and music committees had not even been named yet. They had not had a chance to leak anything, or confront the Prime Minister's ill-natured Philistinism. Perhaps they won't be in the curriculum?

Whistling Flute

My mother delicately
lifted off the ground
a high-pitched flute.

The speed rushed past
and the flute whistled
like a cuckoo humming away.

Mother and father
in the blazing light of the sunset
firing down on them.

Helen, who is 10, wrote this after I'd read the children my puffy, wordy, imprecise prose version of Gerda Mayer's lovely poem 'Fragment' (in *This Way That Way*). The idea comes from Sandy Brownjohn's book, *Does It Have to Rhyme?*

Pauline wrote:

My dad
raised a flute to the sky
on a low hill.

The wind of Wales
puffed some notes
that were yellow, giant and elf
in the moonlight
like a red rose.

We are feeble ghosts
from the ageing years.

A soft beautiful sound.

The children had been asked to take my prose and make a poem of the data it presented, aiming at concision. Afterwards, I read them the Gerda Mayer. They loved it, much as I loved the fact that they had written something strange and new: they had taken the data, and made it theirs.

We held a long-delayed staff meeting on special needs during the first week of the half. Over the past two years we had produced a discussion paper and a policy statement — the former for the teachers facing the review, the latter on demand from the authority. The issue at the meeting was the nature of special needs teaching. I said that children should have more than the basic skills in language.

> *Special Needs Teacher:* The children already do have work in other than the phonics! I often work on maths . . . but work on behavioural problems is beyond my scope, I simply haven't got time for it, and at least one advisory teacher agrees with me . . . children have to know the basic skills before they can read and write . . . Children enjoy the special needs sessions . . .
>
> *Me:* I don't think children should be withdrawn. What do they learn as they walk through the school to the special needs room? That they are special in a way no one would want to be special . . . Why single out SN for its time problem? No one in teaching has time to do a decent job . . . What percentage of the day does each of us spend with each child?
>
> *Tim:* Problems like bereavement, and other special needs — perhaps the class teacher should handle them while the SN teacher takes the class . . .?
>
> *A Teacher:* When the SN teacher works alongside you, it takes a lot of preparation . . . children with special needs require a lot of quiet, the lack of distraction . . . It's all very well talking about the Warnock Act, but its provisions weren't funded . . . We need flexibility. At the moment, some children are withdrawn, and some aren't. That's all right, isn't it ? In any case, I think the children enjoy the time they spend with Evelyn in her room . . .

We agreed at the end of the meeting to form a small group that would write an update of the SN paper by the beginning of February next year. I hoped, though, that flexibility was not merely the licence for any teacher to do what she wanted, what suited her, rather than what suited the children. What about, I thought, doing away with the whole notion of special needs, and simply having another teacher at the children's disposal, to be used as the staff thought best?

'It's not getting any easier yet. We thought it might get better but we think about him all the time . . .' Mrs Andrews read the part about the funeral. Faye sat on the floor of my room playing with a building block, while Ben noisily constructed a car. 'I can't imagine a friendlier school, Mr Sedgwick . . . It was wonderful the way those children spoke to Justin . . . and Mrs Marx . . . It's a lovely school, if we move, we're thinking of moving to Colinsford, where he died at his grandparents', we want Ben to stay here . . .'

She gave me permission to dedicate this book to Justin. 'Are you going to leave Cowper after you've finished this book? . . . We talk about Justin a lot, it would be wrong to pretend he never existed . . .'

Mrs Andrews comes to see me often. I imagine I am yet another link with her son. We talk about schools, and writing, and draw Janice, or Charlotte, or one of the others who knew Justin, into the conversation.

Dear Mr Sedgwick,
In accordance with information fourth year children were requested to note on a letter brought home before half-term a number of parents turned up at the school at 7.30 yesterday evening to attend a High School leavers meeting. As the advice regarding the evening at the High school next week was so late I cannot go to that as I shall be away. So, at much inconvenience, I attended at the school yesterday evening, only to find there was no meeting.

I would have thought that it was an essential ingredient of a child's education to teach 'effective communication' which was sadly lacking regarding this meeting.

Whilst I attended only in case we are not able to find a house and move by next September, which hopefully is unlikely, I do consider that any apology to those parents who did turn up (I saw five) is called for.
Your sincerely

J Carson

Dear Parents,

I must apologise to those of you who came last evening to the meeting that wasn't. This was due to a mix-up between the High School and ourselves, and I greatly regret the mistake.

There will be a meeting on Wednesday November 9th at the High School, and for further information you should ring them on
————.

     I am very sorry for yesterday's error.

Yours sincerely

PS [to Mr Carson] Thank you for your letter. I was very disappointed that your demand for an apology arrived as I was writing one.

Years ago, in another school, I did an assembly about counting out rhymes: 'Eeeny-feeny fithery feg/Deely dyly ham and egg', 'One-ery, two-ery, three-ery, four/I don't love you anymore . . .' and so on. I got them all from one of those books about children's folklore, that risks patronizing, or even disempowering such material by writing it down with footnotes. Still, I wouldn't want to be without the Opies and their kind. I said to the children: 'Have any of you got a rhyme you'd like to share with us?' and 6-year-old Helen chanted clearly to the whole school: 'Ip dip/dogshit/you trod/in it.'

November 1. The decorations are up in the city centre: jolly snowmen and Father Christmasses have been strung across the precincts and the streets, like hanged decadents in a puritan state, since the middle of October. In the school, the first hearing of 'Away in a Manger' was last Wednesday, and Lynda was practising 'Mary Mary' the following day. Outside, though, the grass is covered with autumn leaves, and some are still alive, just about, on the trees. The pollarded birch in the junior courtyard is still green, though beginning to look frayed at the edges, like a dress that's been worn too often. There's a smell of burning in the air. But we are always looking forward to what's coming next, never taking in Now. And what's coming next is Christmas. Coping with that's our next target, our next objective.

    The milkman goes from door to door on the terrace opposite. He glances up at a bedroom window, from which rock music shouts: Craig's big brother is freaking out again. Emma Parkin is in the little room next door to mine, with a bruise the size of two 50p pieces on her right leg. Her mother is coming to see me when she's finished cleaning at The Fisherman's Arms.

    This little room was the deputy's office till the end of July, but when he left, Sue and I changed it into a sitting room: two child-scaled armchairs, paintings on the wall, various building toys, books, comics. Sick children go in there now, rather than wait sadly in the entrance hall with their buckets. The speech therapist, the nurse, the audiologist, the educational psychologist all use it as well, and, at playtimes, Alex, who has broken his arm, builds models in there, accompanied by a friend, who is grateful to Alex for not having to go out in the cold November weather.

The nursery children are in Municipal Park on a trail that Jean and her opposite number as maths co-ordinator at Edinburgh Road have designed. Every class is going eventually, with tasks ahead of them, like counting the number of cirles in climbing frames, estimating distances, and turning 180 degree angles. Many parents are going too, and we hope they will get an opportunity to learn about the teaching of maths, and perhaps see more of what we are trying to do when we emphasize practical experience of number.

Soon there are five children in the little sitting room: Leslie has fallen 'on a bit of orange' and has a lump on his left temple and 'sometimes it goes all funny'; Emma is still waiting to be picked up; Carmel is asleep, having complained of feeling sick; and we can't find mum or dad. And Jonathan has a headache. Most worryingly, Corrine has a puffy bruise going from her left eye, where it is purplish, down to her mouth, where it is blue-grey. It didn't happen at school. We ring her mother at Tesco: 'Oh I thought it might be that . . . we were clowning around yesterday and her face went on the floor. I know it looks terrible, but I can assure you it was a complete accident . . .'

I spent some of today checking old discipline problems. Lee (a problem in April) has calmed down. His work is getting better, and I suspect that he has found that learning to read is not the terror he anticipated, and he is therefore less frustrated, less ready to fling out. As I leave the dinner lady I've been talking with about him, he grins at me.

But Sam, of the tooth abscess and the warring parents, is getting worse. Sometimes we deal with him by letting him do as he likes, as long as it isn't violent. Evelyn, the special needs teacher, comments: 'You have to trade things off with him . . . you make bargains . . . If you do this for me, we'll be able to go out on the playground afterwards . . . If you stand up to him all the time, you get nowhere . . . Even so, though, Fred, he'll have to learn to conform sometime . . .'

Gillian, Evelyn and I agree that the main thing is not to present him with the continuous negative he gets from his mother. But in the back of my mind is the fact that he's approaching that dangerous age, 7, when according to the Jesuits, he'll be lost if he's not won . . .

Carol, his mother, admitted herself to the local mental hospital suddenly, having told the health visitor she was afraid what she might do to Sam. She said she wanted him fostered. A week later, she discharged herself, saying she wanted to keep both boys:

> I want to work with the school but I don't like it that he is treated different from the others, I don't like it that he has his own special desk. He is horrible in the mornings, he is in a vile mood this morning, I had to tell him that if he doesn't behave he doesn't have any Christmas presents this year . . .

Later, Sam draws round his right foot for me:

> 'This is my foot. It is 9 cubes long.'
>
> 'Mrs Brewster, Sam did some lovely work this morning. I always tell you when he's a problem, so I think I ought to tell you when he does something well . . .'
>
> 'I'm surprised, he was terrible this morning . . .'

Luke is 4½. He started the nursery three days ago, and he walks up to me: 'Can you make me a hat?' He is a handsome blond boy, with a little golden ball in the lobe of his left ear. I make him a crown with a piece of card, and put it on his head: 'There. King Luke.' He walks off to show his friends, who all have one.

At 3.50, twenty minutes after school has finished, he is in the little sitting room, playing intermittently with some building equipment. He has not been picked up. Because he was enrolled very late, he isn't in the admissions file. When, after a search, we find his address, we discover he isn't on the phone. He lives over a mile away, in the Bamforth catchment area. I ring them there, in case he is the youngest of a well-known family. 'No, we've no Routledges here.' I also try St Joseph's, in case he's known there, but he isn't. Meanwhile Charlotte is with him, reading stories; but his voice is getting distressed: 'Why isn't my mummy here? When is my mummy coming?'

So Charlotte and I take him home. She sits in the back with him. We are worried too; by now it's half past four, and I would've expected a call from someone. All three of us are thinking, in our different ways, and with different pressures, has anything awful happened? After a complicated journey, and two requests for directions, Luke points: 'That's where I live.' I park the car, jump down to a path, and knock at no.47. 'Mrs Routledge? . . . I've got your little boy . . . no, he's fine . . . in the back of the car . . .'

She comes to the car, full of apologies to Charlotte and me, can't imagine what can have happened, her neighbour was picking him up, she must've forgotten . . . We are just relieved Luke's found his mother. He looks up at her, crying, dying to be picked up and cuddled. 'Why didn't you get me, mummy?' 'Oh, I am sorry Mrs Price . . .'

In final assembly the next Friday, he gets up a minute before the end, the whole school around him, bursts into tears, and runs to the back of the room where his mother is sitting.

Dinner lady: 'Margaret's being foul, Mr Sedgwick. Swearing and kicking me. I can't control her . . . she says Wayne called her a nigger, but she's always saying that, it can't always be true . . .' No, it just often is.

All the building equipment Jean had ordered with the £800 the PTA had raised on the funday was on stage for a Friday assembly. It was mostly girls who had been set free on the advanced stuff, for reasons of positive discrimination. Emma Carson and Sadie Smith had made a car out of Capsula, having conquered two serious morale-threatening construction problems on the way. It zipped along the stage, battery-powered, to the admiration of 360 children. Two boys had made something similar from the same kits, and they had to take a small part from the Emma-Sadiemobile to demonstrate theirs, which went across water.

The nursery children had built a bridge and a train; some lower juniors had made a flower design from plastic nuts, bolts and struts. There was a linked pair of spectacles made from Octons (plastic building shapes) that two girls stood close to each other to wear. Each pair pointed to the other, and bore a legend: I'M WITH THIS IDIOT.

November 8 was so foggy that Helena, from a town fourteen miles away, spent two hours on the journey. Rumour suggested the bonfires — which had spread over five days — had caused the awful visibility. In any case, it was a gift to me with my enlarged non-swimmers group:

Open the Fog

I pull the steel trap, step, to find
a cold whispy shudder of mist.
The white flour is cold and lumpy
and not to taste. Pours out before me.
The freeze melts my face
but no water lies at my feet.
It's a white mirror you cannot touch . . .
Your hand disappears in the light dark . . .
Danielle Price

. . .Fog covers the trees
in a white duvet of dew.

It slides along the ground
and knocks on someone's door and then
whips around the corner . . .
William Skellorn

The fog is thick as a sheepskin.
Sometimes it looks like smashed glass,
like milk spinning . . .
Danuella Whiting

When it comes
cobwebs are just white hair
with hair spray on.
It's a mirror
all smoked up with smoke.
It hits your face
like a spider that has fallen.
You take your glasses off
and everything is blurred.
At night it is like a grey sheet with holes in.

Sarah Woor

Clouds form above my head,
come lower and lower
until they touch
the milk bottle tops . . .
Tiny clouds gather for meetings . . .
But some foglings come
and gather trouble.

Sarah Tobin

It looks like a golfball crushed . . .

Leon Kerry

Every day has its reckoning. Be sure your sins will find you out. There's no pleasure you won't pay for, and no such thing as a free lunch . . .

How those puritan chickens came home to roost today! I'd published in *The Times Educational Supplement* (28 October 1988) a version of my story (see Chapter 2) about Sam, the bad tooth, and the special needs adviser. I'd got the name wrong, for a start: it was the ——————— teacher who'd offended my humanistic sensibilities (and I'm blowed if I'm going to give the correct title here now, for fear of more stressful confrontations). Then the paper's habit of printing at the bottom of articles 'Fred Sedgwick is the head of . . .' didn't help, either, as it sharpened the focus in an entirely unwelcome way.

> *An Authority Figure:* What you wrote about special needs I found offensive in several ways . . . I happen to agree with your thesis . . . but it was telling it like a story that has upset people . . . I'm holding a meeting in an hour's time of the ———————teachers [and I'm blowed again, etc.] and I can assure you your article is pretty high on the agenda . . .
> *Teacher at Cowper:* I was pretty upset by your article, that you didn't tell me about it . . . People said to me, you work at Cowper, do you know about this? . . . and of course I didn't . . .

Another Teacher at Cowper: A lot of your writing is very personal, you know . . . it sometimes feels as if you are the only sensitive person around . . .

A Letter Writer from Lancashire: Just a note to say how much I enjoyed your article about special needs. It's time headteachers started complaining about the service they get . . . Keep up the good work!

Advisory Teacher: I was in York at a conference, and someone waved a copy of your article at me and said, What are you lot doing in ————shire?' I was embarrassed, and pretty cross, I don't mind telling you, Fred . . .

A Phone Call from Dennis: Derby were brilliant Saturday, sorry to hear about City — oh, my teacher who runs a unit here for emotionally troubled kids said, 'Have you seen this?' and it was your article. 'It's brilliant', she said. I said, he's my friend . . .

We've had no break-ins at all since January. In other years, there have been five or six thefts of videos, computers, record-players, fish; or sheer wreckings of offices. In 1988, ex-pupils like Craig or Philip have occasionally clambered on to the roof, and heaved stones at the dome where the majorettes have been practising. But, deplorable as this may have been, the boys were possibly making an aesthetic point, and I take it.

Teachers at Collier Street CP, on the Collier estate, have had two threats of violence over the past three weeks. Cowper's violence, on the other hand, happens at night, in the nearby closes, Cowper itself, Unwin, Bull and the others, when the staff are in their relatively quiet beds in other parts of town. We feel the backwash in the mornings . . .

A report came zigzagging to us about three of our childlren, from two different families, all away one Friday. There'd been screaming in the close at two o'clock in the morning, and threats under the windows of various neighbours. When light came, there was 'kitchen stuff all over the grass on the front lawn . . . all the windows in one house are broken . . . Mrs Mayne is mostly drunk, you see her and her friends around the town with their cans of Carlsberg Special . . . it was frightening during the night . . .'

Another production of the Edinburgh Park Players is coming soon. This is an amateur dramatic society based at Cowper, with members coming from both the staff (Lynda, Iris and now Helena) and the parents. Two weeks before the production, the hall becomes an auditorium, and a set develops on the rudimentary stage the school possesses. The group holds readings and rehearsals intensively throughout the year, but as each play approaches, the production is a more and more prominent topic of conversation in the staffroom.

This term the play is 'The Farndale Women's Institute Dramatic Society's Production of Macbeth', a piece that satirizes, or rather takes the mick out of, amateur dramatics. The play within the play is produced with hamming inefficiency and displays of gargantuan artistic temperament: how can the audience be made certain that those qualities are only in the Farndale WI production, and not in the Edinburgh Park Players?

Lynda is playing Macbeth, and Iris is doubling as First Witch and Macduff. Janice is playing the piano badly — that is, she is making a good job of playing it terribly. The gaudy set is decorated with the word 'MACBETH' illuminated by flashing coloured lightbulbs, and surrounded by plastic ferns and poinsettia. The back cloth is a Scottish vista, all snow-capped mountains and heather. Much of the conversation in the staffroom concerns a disastrous rehearsal, when entries and cues were missed, or how Iris is coping with her two roles. One morning she shows off her talents to the school in assembly, wearing false wig and nose, hamming it up like a disciple of Wolfit:

Round and round the cauldron go;
In the poisoned entrails throw.
Toad, that under cold stone,
Days and nights hast thirty-one . . .

This amazes everybody and delights most. But one nursery girl runs crying to her teacher. Afterwards, Iris disappears for a minute and comes back: 'Will my class stand up please . . .?

I went to the first night, as president of the group. Bryan, one of our governors, was in charge of sound and the lights. The hall was crowded, and the laughter appreciative. Everything was done for laughs: gay jokes, short-sighted jokes, cripple jokes. Iris kept appearing at the wrong cues, with her quavering line, 'Thrice the brinded cat has mewed . . .', to be bundled off the stage with increasing ferocity by the other women. She was very funny, haring round the cauldron on crutches, then later in a wheelchair. She was just doing her job as well as she could, not hamming it up at all. This is like her teaching: unspectacular, professional, and, finally, extremely effective. Janice accompanied the witches in a spirited version of 'That Old Black Magic'. Lady Macbeth was played by a very tall man in drag, and the audience loved it all.

To Social Services
Dear ————,
As promised on the telephone to your Mrs Bakewell, I append our notes about Margartet Newton of 72 Cowper Close (date of birth 20/1/78)

11/11/88 Late. 'Overslept —no one to wake me up.'

15/11/88 Arrived 11.25 am claiming she'd been at the dentist's and will have to wear a brace.

Said at weekends she has to look after her auntie's baby 'and it's terrible, the baby always screams when she goes out.'

16/11/88 Teacher had to ring home to get Margaret into school on time for planned trip to bird reserve.

21/11/88 Very cold day — M has no overcoat or anorak, and is wearing sandals.

22/11/88 M claimed a pair of gloves were hers when they almost certainly weren't.

We are very worried about this child. She is emotionally unstable, and we fear she has too great a weight to bear in terms of responsibility at home.

By the way, we found out that she didn't have an appointment at the dentist's. We would value your advice.

Yours sincerely

Simon is a parent governor, and he is keen to see the children working with the building equipment the PTA have bought with Jean's advice and £500 from the summer fair profits. Possibly he had been sceptical of its value at the time. In any case, he is in Anna's class of middle infants, where Miriam is due to start as new deputy head in January. I made notes on this occasion.

Two boys have used something called ASCO to build a rigid shape. 'It was Lennie who finally worked out that you needed struts across the thing to make it firm', says Anna. Then Simon helps Lennie put wheels on with nuts and bolts. Andrew (who almost never says anything) is there. 'That's lovely Andrew — what are you making?' 'Rocket.' Anna helps Ricky put his shoes on: 'I think you've got thicker socks today, Ricky.'

In this room: thirty children, one governor, teacher, classroom ancillary, head.

Anna worries to me: her contract ends this term — should she apply for other jobs or go for supply at Cowper? She hasn't been well — perhaps more intermittent work would suit better . . .?

Lewis has made a model: wine box, toilet roll middles, red stripe painted carefully down it: 'It's a jam sandwich.' 'Jam sandwich?' 'Here's the boot . . . .' 'Do you mean it's a police car?' 'Yeah, yeah.'

Andrew is talking, talking. Animatedly. To a friend, a girl, by the coathooks the other side of the room . . .

. . . In Lorna's room, Simon helps three boys with Kugeli . . . Children are drawing with the Nimbus computer. Susie and Jimmy (who has just recovered from a meningitis scare) are building with Super Octons: Jimmy says, 'I have made a spaceship' and Susie: 'I'm building two feet upside down.' Jen says, when I ask her: 'I don't know what I am building.'

In Iris's room, they are making police cars out of Lego. The penny drops about the jam sandwich: the police liaison officer is here, and has been in the school for two days. 'We call them jam sandwiches', she says.

'This is the red light at the front. This is the red roof. The bits keep falling of. Have you seen Chrissie's? . . . Chrissie, do you need those wheels?'

'Yeah. No. You can have 'em. Here, you can have these wheels . . .'

'Geoffrey, mine keeps breaking up . . .'

'Mine don't. It's more better.'

Shaun has made a machine gun from some mint condition wooden building materials. A-a-a-a-a-a-a-a. He shoots me down.

Dennis rang:

> A kid swallowed a pin today . . . a sewing pin . . . Why is it always, 'Send for Dennis' when things like this happen? The other week the caretaker collapsed in the hall, and they all said, 'Send for Dennis' . . . Why is this? What do they think I can do that they can't? This kid with the pin, I'd no more idea what to do about it than anyone else . . .?

Dennis's liberal soul recoils from an economic reality: he is paid more than anyone else. Sally objects to this: 'Would you not want to know if someone had swallowed a pin?' 'I wouldn't give a damn, as long as everyone was all right . . .' But I know that the highest paid carries the can and gets the drinks in: when I suggest that the three students should celebrate their success with a bottle or two on Friday, Charlotte says: 'The highest paid should buy the wine . . .'

One student, Maggie, played guitar and piano in assembly within her first week. The three of them perform well with children and teachers, and only show outright anxiety when they know their tutor is coming. Tim comments after one such visit: 'The style hasn't changed much since St Luke's in 1968.'

Lynda gave me a cheque for £200, the proceeds from the Scotttish play. She auctioned the props for school funds: two bloody daggers, two clean ones; a tree; several crowns; several witches' hats; a few ghosts on sticks; a handful of swords; lots of string. The children went home happily. The £200 will go towards a new computer.

I asked the non-swimmers to write a poem expressing their feelings about someone they disliked, believing that poetry is one place (unlike, for example, assembly halls, playgrounds and classrooms) where all feelings are legitimate. Danielle wrote:

> As I slide off my sock
> and open every window in the house,
> the puff goes miles.

As I run fast
my heart is beating
like a copper penny.

My eyes sting with anger:
I'll get you for that!

I'll take out my glass eye
and throw it at you:
Whizz!

Yes, and it will hit
your big bum

and it will be so red
it will burn in the blazing fire.

You stink
I say in red anger.

All I get back,
not a stick
but a great tree trunk.

Stay away from him awhile.

I think my nose is so cold
it's going to drop off
and all the snot in the world
I will throw at you.

I will give a big puff
and the world will stop turning
Space will fall at my feet
and I will warm my snotty nose.

Mark, who has had problems, as a bully, and because he frequently smells bad, has been away for four weeks after an operation on an undescended testicle. On his first day back, I see him on his own at 8.10 am at a bus stop as I drive to school.

A visit from a party of fifty Americans, three years ago, has passed into the folklore of Cowper. They found our school so, so creative. Most of them were teachers, but some had brought spouses with them to see Europe. They also brought gifts: shoe polish, a biro with a transparent barrel that contained a shredded dollar bill, brochures about Manhattan. No jazz records or bottles of rye, though. The leader of the party said to me, as she handed over a bag with these 'goodies for the natives' (Tim): 'I guess you're not too fond of us just at the moment.' This was days after the Tripoli raid.

Indeed the occasion did give rise to a ferocious anti-Americanism in some of the staff. I asked one colleague, a CND member, if all our jokes about Yanks weren't racist: 'Yes. But the Americans *are* awful.' The leader of the group enrolled me as a member of the International Association for Childhood Education as she got back on the coach. 'That was a very beautiful experience . . .' I have the lapel stud still.

An elderly non-teacher gentleman and his wife were in the nursery:

'Say, look at this big bowl of brown sugar . . .'
'That's sand, Art. That's sand.'

Dear ————,
I am in the later stages of preparing for print a book about a year in the life of a school (called in the book Cowper School) and would be grateful for permission to use, anonymously, some correspondence of yours.

To save you the trouble of a reply, your signature at the bottom of this letter would suffice if you are agreeable — though correspondence is always welcome!
Yours sincerely

Dear Boys and Girls in Mrs Noah's class,
I'm glad to hear you enjoy my poem 'The First Lick of the Lolly' . . . I heard too that you've been reading some of my riddles, so I thought I would send you a new one . . .

I am a see-through pear
Hanging from my treeless branch,
A bit of a conjurer I can ripen suddenly,
Or disappear at a switch.
Like the apple I am good for you
Lengthening your days.

All best wishes and take care,

John Cotton

Lynda rang at 4.00 pm after another day in the West Country:

> I got the job . . . There was just me and this other girl . . . They made me play the piano! 'Praise Him' . . . I just opened the hymnbook and played . . . They've got walk-in stock cupboards, things would be a lot easier at Cowper if we had walk-in stock cupboards! The staff seem very quiet. I'd like a day down there to meet the children, perhaps in the spring, I hope that'll be OK . . .

Lynda had had four interviews, and when she got back home from the successful one, she found a letter on the doormat asking her to another. As she's been here eleven years, this will be a watershed in the life of the school. She has run large parts of the staff's social life, like the Edinburgh Road Players and the end of term celebrations. She has controlled the art and craft resources and much of the teaching. She knows everybody's culinary preferences and their star signs. She is always the first to know any new baby's birth weight. As a fine cook, she is much valued as a hostess. But she will be remembered most for her kindness and her energy. Someone said, 'If anyone's in trouble, you can be sure Lynda will be first on the scene.'

Reading the above in draft, one of her colleagues said, 'Lynda is emerging in your book as the tart with the heart.'

> The Headmaster
> St Bernard's College
> Dear Sir,
> I heard of an incident that took place yesterday which has caused considerable distress here, and I know you would wish to be informed.
>
> Following a football match at your school, which my team greatly enjoyed, despite losing heavily, several of my boys were insulted by yours with cries of 'Blacky' and 'Nigger'. One of my boys was struck in the face, and had to be restrained from running after your boys. The St Bernard's boy who hit my boy was not one of those involved in the game.
>
> A girl who was playing was also subject to jibes from spectators.
>
> Both these children are away from school this morning. We try hard to teach children that whatever colour or sex people are, we treat them the same, and we are distressed to find much of our teaching in this area brought to nothing by an experience of this kind.
> Yours sincerely

There was no reply to this, but the games master came round — once to express incredulity, and again to tell us the boys concerned had been punished.

'Of course we can't have her here!'

'Why not?'

'Because she's obviously an extreme left wing candidate.'

'What is your evidence for that?'

'She believes in mixed ability teaching, and she calls herself "Ms".'

'But this authority's policy has been mixed ability for years!'

'Then this authority's policy is wrong, and must be changed.'

The speakers in this anecdote are, first, a county councillor, and second, an adviser. It comes from another authority. But it could happen anywhere, now that, as the adviser said to me in the saloon bar of the —————shire Arms, decisions that affect children's education and teachers' careers are made on the basis of gossip about whether somebody is 'one of us'.

Charlotte, one morning in late November: 'Have you ordered the Christmas tree yet?' It can't be put off any longer — so the caretaker rings the local garden centre.

MEANIES

Education lecturer Mary Drummond and headmaster Fred Sedgwick want schools to drop nativity plays.

They claim the tinsel glitter and cardboard haloes don't reflect Christmas realities of poverty.

WHAT A PAIR OF MISERIES!

Christmas is supposed to be a time of joy, not despair.

Children love being in nativity plays. Parents enjoy seeing them.

LET'S RAISE THE CURTAIN.

— Editorial in *The Sun,* December 1987.

Mary Jane Drummond and I had published an article in *Junior Education* in November 1987 arguing that most school Christmasses brought about a serious degeneration of the standard of children's experiences, with templates, sentimental songs and interminable rehearsals, during which most children sat about on the hall floor waiting for hometime. The article ended: 'This year, let's have some work that accepts the reality of the Bethlehem event as it probably was. Refugee. Pregnant. Rejected. The proud scattered in the imagination of their hearts. There's some raw material there, surely?'

Nobody had noticed this piece except the *Daily Telegraph,* who had telephoned me at school about it. ('Is Mary Drummond Miss or Mrs?' 'I think Ms would be best.' 'We don't use that expression at the *Telegraph.*') The next day this appeared:

. . . Productions should avoid stereotyped portrayals of women, husbands and rulers, Miss Drummond and Mr Sedgwick advised . . .

Parents' ideas of a traditional Christmas usually betrayed 'Victorian attitudes' towards women and the Christian faith . . . the realities of the first Christmas had instead been 'poverty, homelessness and childbirth'. Primary school children were unable to understand the incarnation but they could look at babies, presents and parenthood, viewing such subjects 'vividly, dramatically and drawing on their own living experiences . . .' Mr Sedgwick said yesterday he wanted schools to transmit what he called the central message of Christmas: 'That God became Man through people of low degree.'

This fair piece was linked to another, beginning, almost self-parodyingly: 'A lesbian version of Cinderella . . .'

Then a parent showed me *The Sun* editorial ('You can't be all bad, if you've been attacked by that lot, Mr Sedgwick'), and there was a piece in *Today*. Local TV and radio interviewed Mary Jane and me, and cameras filmed rehearsals for Cowper's production. I told Radio Ulster Mary Jane's Hackney story:

'Is Father Christmas coming this year, Miss?'
'Of course, Maxie. He comes every year.'
'Well, he didn't come last year.'

An ITV journalist asked 9-year-old Christopher: 'What do you think of Mary going all that way on a donkey?'. 'It's terrible — what if her waters had broken!'

Mary Jane and I had certainly touched a nerve. In cynical moments we reflected that a traditional Christmas was important in schools because it stopped education going on. The curriculum roundabout jolted to a halt, and everybody sang 'Silent Night' in candlelight, having dabbed paint through templates of wise men, shepherds and the baby Jesus.

Little Donkey

Little Donkey, little donkey,
On the dusty road,
Get a move on, little donkey,
Boring little toad.

Been a long time, little donkey,
I've been standing here.
Wonder if the staff would notice
If I grabbed a beer.

Pour me a Bells tonight
Rose and Crown, Rose and Crown.
I'll need a few tonight
On the town,
On the town.

Little donkey, little donkey,
had a heavy night:
Seven pints, I'm walking homeward,
Not a pretty sight.

Little donkey,
Little donkey,
Not a pretty sight.

English for ages 5 to 11 arrived. I turned to section 10, on writing, and was encouraged: they've taken up Frank Smith's distinction between the secretarial and the compositional aspects of writing, and they warn us against over-correction of mistakes. But there is a basic contradiction. Paragraph 10.19 pulls the rug from the National Curriculum's target structure when it says: 'The best writing is vigorous, committed, honest and interesting. We have not included these qualities in our attainment targets because they cannot be mapped on to levels . . .' But there follows the usual table of targets that cannot, by the committee's own admission, begin to comprehend what really matters in writing. It reduces everything to a banal behaviouristic taxonomy.

Daniel, singing absent-mindedly: "'The Christmas Tree, the Christmas Tree/The lights do shine so prettily . . ." Mrs Rowell put a line through Jason's work because it didn't make sense . . . I think they ought to put a line through The Christmas Tree, because that doesn't make sense either.'

One day Tim's class did a fine assembly on Divali with John, the student. They lit lamps, they told the story of Rama and Sita, they held up Rangooli patterns.

Later, 5-year-old Lenny, from Donna's class, made a Christmas card for his older brother and sister, who are at high school. Donna sent a verbal message with him to Lynda: 'How do you spell Aaron and Syreeta?' Lenny and his friend returned twenty minutes later with a piece of paper with John's handwriting on it: 'Divali'.

School is full of absurd experiences like this, but usually only the children see them for what they are. This time, as I said to Tim, we had Donna on the ropes.

The Journey
Mary sat on the donkeys back and rested then the baby started to kick and Mary started to say stop Joseph and Joseph stopped, and said Mary calm down. Calm down. So Mary calmed down. The Joseph turned and the donkey went peacefully into the moonlight.

Mark (8)

Bank Manager Visits Jesus

He enters the stable, briefcase,
waistcoat and jacket,
looking down at the baby,
gold to his eyes.
Joseph is singing 'A penny for a rhyme'.
He looks at Mary crying with joy,
her tears pound coins,
the straw shreds of five pound notes,
Jesus a fortune lying in a manger
made of bronze, put together
with silver shining needles.

Pauline (10)

The second of these was brought about by using an idea of Jill Pirrie's from her book, *On Common Ground* (Hodder and Stoughton).

Why is he like this? He won't do anything I ask him to do . . . In our house, it's pyjamas at half past five, then playing at six, then quiet time at half past six, then bed at seven. Sometimes he's awake and messing about at one or two in the morning! No, I can't share my time with him . . . he wants to watch television and I want to play my records . . . I don't like all this special treatment he's getting at school — the others aren't allowed their own special place to sit, they don't go to see Mr Sedgwick every time they do something right . . . I don't want him treated special . . .

Carol is talking about Sam to the educational psychologist, who had tested him in the little room next to mine, and been surprised when he'd produced an Old Spice deodorant stick and applied it to his armpits. Though where else he might have applied it wasn't suggested. He behaved very well 'considering', the psychologist said, 'his reputation'. She suspected he wouldn't last long in normal schools, not because of anything inside him, as his mother believed, but because of the repressive regime she ran.

The house in Cowper Close is immaculate, and more or less any act of Sam's either disrupts something his mother has just tidied, or breaks a rule she has laid down. Often it does both. She agrees with Evelyn that he'll have to conform one day, but she is puritanical in her insistence that it should be, at the latest, tomorrow. Meanwhile, Sam improves in school, barking less loudly at lunchtimes, almost peaceable on the playground, and learning to read and write. His drawing is careful and imaginative. He is happy at Cowper.

Interviews for the new caretaker, the visit of City Football team . . . these were the main items on a Monday agenda that also included teaching the non-swimmers and a lunchtime fancy dress disco in the dome. I explained to the candidates and their wives (who are also invited, because the post is residential) about the day: City FC, disco and all:

> I thought you'd like to see the school as it is, with a lot going on . . .
> I've never seen schools as cathedrals, and you'll see a lot of paint around
> the school . . . art is very important to young children . . . we do
> teach children to clear up after a day's work, but there is a lot for
> caretaker and cleaners to do at Cowper . . . the hall is in use most
> evenings for various lettings, and of course the caretaker is in charge for
> all of that . . .

One of the candidates murmured to me as we began the trip round the school, 'Thanks very much, I've seen what I want, I think I'll call it a day now.' And then there were four.

School lunch was cheese salad. The candidates, Jimmy Randle (from the office) and I sat with the children, till I broke up the uncomfortable party to see how the disco was progressing. . .

About twenty children were in there, fancily-dressed: tramps, dolls, cricketers, clowns, robots, rabbits. We stopped the dancing for a moment, and they paraded round the room while the winners were chosen by Jimmy Randle, here officially to interview the candidates, and me. After lemonade and prizes, more children arrived with their entrance money (20p, for school fund) and the dancing, under the supervision of Janice and almost all the rest of the staff, continued. Two of the candidates looked in.

Then, on time, the manager of City FC arrived. I met him on the path outside my room and saw how tired he looked after his well publicized trip to eastern Europe to buy new players. As soon as I'd told him where the team was to practise, he called out in Scots accent utterly unsoftened by fifteen years in English League football, 'Right. Come on. This way', and the players decanted themselves from cars: the six-foot-four goalkeeper who'd dropped the ball before our appalled eyes at an opposing forward's feet the previous Saturday; the old City player who'd had his glory days with Liverpool, and who was now with us again, on his way down; the 'commanding central defender' who'd been sent off against Manchester City; the redheaded 'terrier-like midfielder' the manager had found playing for Scunthorpe; the tall winger — 'silky-skilled', the local paper always called him — who came from the secondary school we can see over the main road, and who's going to play for England one day . . .

All this lot, plus eight others, ran on to the field. They were polite and charming: decent young men probably grateful for a gift nobody can explain, that's saved them from painting and decorating, hod-carrying, caretakership, office work, small business, teaching, unemployment . . . being bored, or distressed or suicidal . . . They sprinted, stood in a circle, passed to each other, chasing their passes across the diameter of the circle; they tackled and dribbled, while the whole school stood and watched, with varying degrees of interest. I went in to begin the interviews.

Photograph 3: The footballers visit Cowper   Photo courtesy of the *Evening Star*

Tim told me afterwards:

They played a game, City versus the children . . . and of course the children won . . . One of the nicest things — I would've needed a telephoto lens to catch it — was when the City team got a perfect cross in and one of them aimed at it — he could've put it anywhere he wanted — and nodded it gently right into Robert's arms. Robert'll never forget that . . .

Inside, we were slowly developing a picture of an appointment: Mr Barry Martin, an Aston Villa supporter from Wolverhampton.

Some quotations from the candidates:

I don't think I could do maintenance, I could just about do a plug, someone would have to show me how to do the rest . . . My husband will help, though . . . I like children, I get on well with the staff, all my kids have been here, it's a happy school, I'd like to come here. I've enjoyed being a cleaner and a dinner lady — I've been a cook as well, and I'd like to offer what I can as caretaker . . .

I can't pretend I know anything about caretaking, but I get on with people. I speak my mind, I enjoy a good argument with management at the Post Office, but the Post Office is dead now with what they're asking you to do . . . We're in a caravan at the moment, and as you probably noticed my wife is pregnant, and we'd like very much to live in the bungalow . . .

There's a lot to be done here . . . I think the vandalism's gone down because we talk to the locals, we don't just tell them off . . . [wife of the last caretaker, who is going on to senior management in the service]

My present school has a judge as chairman of the governors . . . the standard of this school's cleanliness? . . . Well, it has a lot of potential. I've been caretaking for a long time, my dad was a caretaker, Sir . . . I tried selling insurance for a couple of years but it didn't work out . . . My in-laws live in this town and I feel at home here even though I've lived all my life in Wolverhampton . . .

Photograph 4: Donna's children wearing home-made hats

Photo courtesy of Terry Kenny

Roast turkey, cooked by the new classroom ancillary; an array of garlicky salads; a nut roast; a lasagne; a flan; french bread and butter; fruit, profiteroles, gateaux, cream; sherry ('Thank you for all your support during the term I've been acting — Janice'); red wine, white wine: it's the Christmas dinner again. The nursery staff, remembering the jolly pecker Don gave them last year, have a present for him: ('regular exercise creates a stronger, bigger, more beautiful love muscle . . . men "pump iron" all over the world for bigger biceps, stronger shoulders and calves, trimmer waists — a more beautiful body with more stamina — but one vital part of the body has not been catered for . . . until now . . .').

Afterwards children's parties are everywhere: rowdy games, best clothes, mums and the occasional dad helping with the celebrations. Twiglets, sandwiches and jellies, sausages on sticks. The year dies. A few dead leaves hang, and the trees are arthritic fingers. Litter persists, despite the demise of the tuck shop. I've got a cold. Mrs Bennet, the crossing patrol, goes off in luminous white, yellow and orange. The children will be excited as they go home.

One of the polystyrene and plaster sculptures Lynda's class made with Emmanuel is in my room still, chipped and the worse for wear following its journeys: first to the Burns Elliot Hall, and then to Leamington Spa, to be photographed for Lynda's article for *Art and Craft*. It's a stool, and it's holding up a flowing spider plant I use for drawing when I'm suddenly called on to teach. Whenever I look at it, I think of Emmanuel and all we did together: the first planning meeting with Liz from the local Arts Association; the plaster-littered sessions in the libary; all the joyful conversations; the exhibition in the Burns Elliot Hall; and that final assembly: 'I was a flower, a blossoming flower . . .'

My room is heftily decorated with Christmas cards, too, that I'll take home, an hour or so after school ends. There are presents for me as well: one will be a packet of orange chocolate sticks, the other a bottle from the Sainsbury Vintage Collection.

From the hall comes the sound of children cheering, and the banal pump of pop as they dance the last dance.

Afterword

. . .it is the business of education to make us freer and more creative. (Lawrence Stenhouse, *An Introduction to Curriculum Design and Development*, Heinemann)

Fortunately, in England at any rate, education produces no effect whatsoever. If it did, it would prove a serious danger to the upper classes, and probably lead to acts of violence in Grosvenor Square. (Wilde, *The Importance of Being Earnest*)

Just as the metaphor of the market dominates and distorts the government's understanding of society as a whole, so the metaphor of delivery dominates and distorts its understanding of education. Indeed the two metaphors are essentially the same. (Michael Armstrong, 'Popular Education and the National Curriculum' in *Forum*)

this is bandit country amigo
& the bandits are in office (Michael Blackburn, 'Hombre's Advice', from *Backwards into Bedlam*)

I sat in the chair pointed out to me, and faced a line of agreeable people: all sweaters, open-necked collars, jeans, denim shirts, welcoming smiles, frank eyes. A *Guardian* peeped from the odd pocket, a moth or two may have floated up. The questions were of the kind any candidate should welcome: easy to answer, but revealing. 'Tell me about some work you've done that you're particularly pleased with . . . What should a special needs policy look like? . . . How do you help the head deal with a weak teacher? . . . I see you have an interest in drama — how do you foster your own specialism in a school?' I battled on happily enough, secure in the knowledge that I was in a thin short story, one that did not convince me, even in a fictional sense, and that I did not have to worry about.

When it ended, I turned the chair ninety degrees, so I could lead the discussion for the whole group: including, now, a line that I had not yet seen. The first three on the left were men: ties knotted as small as I'd ever seen ties seriously knotted, Adam's apples crushed; clipboards on knees, paper filled with notes. The women wore suits, too, and tie-aping floppy bows — not to be outdone in the managerial stakes.

The men said to the other group, as I kicked off the evaluation discussion (for, if it hasn't been clear up to now, let me make it clear at this point: this was role play, a charade):

'You didn't really tear the candidate apart.'
'You've got to really hammer the candidate.'
'When I get a deputy I expect to burn him out and send him on to a headship.'

(quoted in *The Times Educational Supplement*, 9 August 1985)

I was helping to run a course on primary management. My job in this mixture of role play, lectures and discussion groups had been to submit an application for a deputy headship, to be interviewed by a group of participants on the course, and to chair a discussion with the group. As I'd waited in the draughty corridor, I'd regretted signing the application form with a silly name. 'Mr Grovel — would you like to come in now, please?'

A year earlier, I'd interviewed two headteachers — both male, again — about how they had, or were about to, change their schools. The head who was beginning said, in the summer holidays before he took up his appointment:

I've already started. I sat at the back of everyone's class and made notes . . . I wanted them to be afraid of me . . . there are some tough cookies there, they have to be come down on hard . . . They have to be made afraid. In the final analysis that school is mine, and if I give them the toy of democracy, it won't work . . .

He called a staff meeting before term began and re-designated everyone's scale posts (this story is pre-Main Professional Grade). I asked him how the teachers had responded: 'They were tight-lipped, wary . . . They were stunned, they were silent. They accepted it . . . I said, I'll tell you what I want you to know . . .'

The other head had been in post for seven years when he described to me certain changes he'd made in his school:

I said this is how I want it done and that's purely it . . . When I said I want the children in groups they went in groups. Streaming went. That was another thing I changed immediately, I didn't even have any discussion about that. 'Streaming is going', I said . . . I got the impression they were happy with the changes . . . The grouping wasn't open to question, they were going to go like that, whether the staff liked it or not . . .

(quoted in *The Times Educational Supplement,* 2 May 1986)

These anecdotes (collected during research for an MA degree in 1984) are relevant to the Cowper story because they speak about the vital (and nowadays largely clouded) issue of the ownership of the school. In the perspective these speakers share, the school belongs to the head: at one point this is quite explicit: 'In the final analysis that school is mine.' But it is implicit everywhere else, most chillingly in that remark about 'the toy of democracy'.

The other chill in these stories is in the violence of the imagery: 'tear apart'; 'hammer'; 'burn out'; 'afraid'; 'come down on hard'; 'stunned': the strong, even the aggressive, shall inherit the world of educational management in the 1990s: those who are capable of a reign of terror without too much loss of sleep: the Pinochets of educational management.

I had noted early in my research for this book how violent imagery recurred in talk about education. Indeed, my account of the year begins with a story of a fight between two parents; and throughout the year, on and off, children scrapped in the playground like figures in a Lowry painting (at least as seen from my room). The working title for the book was 'The Good Fight'.

These realities underwrote for me a larger, more serious fight that was going on without the triviality that usually marks children's quarrels — at least as perceived by adults. This was the constant skirmishing between a view of education that sees schools as socio-technical institutions where cost-effectiveness is central to their lives; where, as Michael Armstrong says, 'the market dominates and distorts'; and where participants have to be managed to a technocratically optimum state; or, in contrast, as places where the humanity of individuals is celebrated as they negotiate — not only timetables, spending and power over the curriculum, but their very realities, the ways in which they recreate the image of God in themselves.

The technocrats are, of course, in the ascendant, with their view of 'training' to be 'delivered', disregarding thousands of years of thought that shows how a Socratic model of conversation, of dialogue, rather than of lecture, is the way in which human beings come to terms with their own nature and the world around them — not to mention the complex relationship between the two. Instrumentalist views of the curriculum predominate in the priorities implicit in the way the National Curriculum is being built, with maths, science and a slightly coarse view of language first, second and third, and arts, politics, humanities, nowhere.

In its crudest terms, this view of education is put, by a writer in *The Times Educational Supplement,* thus:

Why do the educational establishments refuse to listen when their customers, the employers, tell them that *what* they are producing is not what is required? . . . Are students being prepared for life in industry where the system of control is dictatorial? . . . we need people who will take orders, not give them . . . An education system . . . is essentially *a routine batch exercise . . .* [my italics]

This writer does not believe that schools are there to serve society, but to service small engineering firms (one of which he runs). His is an extreme statement of instrumentalism, but it is widely held by many in his position, and is not so far removed from the views of Government ministers. I noted how the Prime Minister, during the year in which I was logging the life of Cowper School, denied the very existence of society: something to whose survival we all might have a duty; something whose variety, in cultural, religious and racial terms, we might all celebrate. If society does not exist, we are back to the survival of the economically fittest.

For the writer quoted above, and for the Prime Minister, the ability to take orders is what schooling must inculcate. The words of their rhetoric are 'train', 'skills', 'efficiency', 'delivery', 'market forces' and 'benchmarks'. The view of education that manages to recognize, let alone celebrate, humanity, sees as central to schools the ability to debate, to question. The priority here is the preservation of democracy, of the individual's confused interaction with his world.

Look: Leslie has slipped on a bit of orange peel, and his head keeps going all funny; Luke is crying because his mother's friend has forgotten to pick him up, and the November night is very dark; Justin is remembered daily in the autumn, looking at a watch, smiling under a white cap, there to disguise the effects of radiotherapy; Sue the secretary has left, and we have no replacement; somebody from Cowper has stolen a medal from a museum on a bright summer day; Carol has glue in her eye and thinks she's blind; Darren has enjoyed a week in the Lake District; Margaret wants to stay there, among the calm of the hills and her teachers' patient care; Emmanuel has turned up at last, and is having his photograph taken by *The Times Educational Supplement's* freelance; Sue is late because her daughter won't walk to school dressed as a French waitress; Anthony's shoes are two sizes too small for him, and he has no teddy to cuddle when I take him home on a damp spring afternoon; Jenny says assemblies are just like her grandad's funeral; there's a fight on the playground, under the half-wrecked silver birches; and there's another one: two women, a long time ago, last winter, during a governors' meeting . . .

One parent asked me at a later governors' meeting whether there was any objection to a school council, and this made me question again, and more seriously, whether the school belonged to any of that list: head, LEA, DES, voter, tax-payer, parents, industry, teachers. The children, meek or otherwise, will inherit whatever world we leave for them, and the school is theirs in the most real sense: it exists solely for their benefit. The Plowden Report was called *Children and THEIR* [my emphasis] *Primary Schools.*

What'll happen next year? The National Curriculum and Local Management will arrive. We will learn more about competition . . . but at Cowper, regardless of any of this, the children will still be helped to express themselves, through poetry, art, music, scientific exploration — and a school council? Whatever happens, the trend towards greater autonomy for the real owners of Cowper must continue.

What do ex-progressives get in the way of support, and advice on how to cope with new political realities? I went to a lecture by an ex-ILEA head, and made notes.

We are offered Chinese proverbs we warmed to at College, twenty years ago: 'I listen and I forget, I see and I remember, I do and I understand'; we are given lists of thinkers down the centuries who would have agreed with us: Plato, Ascham, Rousseau, Piaget. Thick gruel, but thin comfort. They've all said things like 'Unless a child does, he will not understand.' or 'As I talk, I create.' We are given sympathetic agreement with our worries — that as teachers we are being de-professionalized, and our children made into fodder for factories and offices; that the service we have worked in for years is being deliberately destabilized, so that our local education authorities can be destroyed as inefficient, and the work they do now privatized, as though they sold soapflakes.

But what does all this agreement mean to me, as I come from school, with Sam's problems, and fears about tomorrow? . . . after twenty minutes concentrated diplomacy between a parent and a teacher? Lecturers with progressive persuasions say about the National Curriculum, 'It's not thought out', and then, 'it's elitist.'

But perhaps it is all too carefully thought out: if the Government intends the disempowerment of state schools, it will spend peanuts on resources and thinking, and that's what has happened. It will then watch as the middle class drifts towards private education. Some schools — Cowper among them — will be left with ethnic minorities and what sociologists in the USA still call 'the poor working class'. The conclusions are inescapably political: Margaret, Luke, Anthony, Damien, Mark and the others are to be separated from the children whose parents can afford private education. Educational reform is being used to increase social divisions.

The heirs of the 1960s progressive movement look like an elderly Habitat interior: all hessian, good taste and shocked avoidance of contemporary reality. They cannot meet the challenge of the competitive ideology that has won the hearts and minds of the middle classes, because they believe in the essential goodness of humankind. They do not like the notion of the good fight, with its ugly militaristic metaphors, but it is hard to see how justice will be won back for Margaret and the children at Cowper while they are on a slide towards decreased resources, dirty buildings, poorly paid teachers and a joylessly instrumentalist curriculum.

The progressive movement of the 1960s hardly affected reality then. Schools where the child was the centre of the educational process were rare. Any offering of autonomy to children happened spasmodically and, essentially, patronizingly: here and there a classroom that measured up to Clegg's *The Excitement of Writing,* or the Plowden Report, or (in the 1970s) the Humanities Curriculum Project. But in 1981 I worked in a school that had not had the 1960s, let alone the 1980s, and from my experience there were plenty of these around.

Progressivism only appeared, first, in the colleges of education, as a way forward, and, second, in the editorials of the *Daily Mail,* as an ideology to be attacked to stop us thinking about the failing economy, or the disasters, both actual and potential, of world politics, or the public safety of the people. Now progressivism looks even more threadbare: the hessian discoloured, the displays frayed; in need of a long look at what really happens in school, not at what cultivated middle-class educators would like to happen.

This book is an attempt to look at what occurred in and around one school in 1988. I would like to think it is research, but I suspect there is not enough of other perspectives in it for it to aspire to such high status: what does that angry parent think? or that officer? Also, my PhD tutor would comment on the lack of references, and the paucity of theory generated by my data. But nevertheless, I am a teacher-researcher, offering my perspective, hoping that the business of reflecting on Cowper's practice in 1988, and writing about it, will help me make my work as an educator better.

I have tried to avoid a fault that a tutor picked out in my work on a course eight years ago. I was writing about games teaching at my last school: it was all too competition-biased for my taste, and I said so, outlining what games lessons ought to look like. The tutor wrote, 'this is fine, but the trouble is that you emerge as the most sensitive and intelligent person in the school. This may well be the case, of course, but it is not the job of research to say it . . .' At times during the writing of this book I have bent over too far, some readers of my typescript say, to give the opposite impression: 'You do', said one, 'paint a rather dark picture of yourself.'

It is not fiction, because everything happened, either at Cowper, or at other schools where I was head. The names have been changed to offer a kind of fictional distance; to help me to see the events I've written about in an approximation to an objective way. In any case, I have been too political for fiction. Art cannot wear so vulnerably its heart on its sleeve. But who can respond to a massive political initiative, like the legislation of the 1980s, without being political?

What I have produced is a kind of journalism, written with a confessed belief: that what good things there are in the world should be open to all, like Emmanuel's art: that Margaret, and Damien, and Mark, and Danielle and all the children in Cowper Close, are owed, in the name of justice, whatever can be given them. That a just society will not whittle away their chances because of what their fathers and mothers do not earn. That teachers have a duty to offer the best, regardless of ephemera like what is cost-effective in the marketplace of the late 1980s.

If I have emerged from this exercise with admiration for anyone, it is for the teachers I work with: Lynda and her sheer industry, and her determination, her resilience in the face of failure; Jean, Iris and Janice, for their ability to change intellectually and professionally at a latish stage, and their humane view of how we might face the centralization of education; Tim and his kindness towards every child, occasionally contrasting with his staffroom cynicism;

Barbara and her religious love of the world, which means work; Jeanette, Helena and Donna, with their young people's idealism; Don and his good humour; Gillian and her reliability; Charlotte, with her keen sense of justice and democracy; Lorna and Evelyn for their commitment to the children whom life appears to have served a raw deal; the deputy for his humour and talent . . .

Sometimes it seems to me that the job of headship today is to stand between these people and the crasser effects of managerialism. However much headteachers are swamped with those 'useless bits of paper', their function is to keep their schools human, funny and open places where Sally, the nursery nurse, who is a teacher in every sense except one, is as respected professionally as everyone else: places where a parent could say (as Mrs Andrews did say to me last week), 'You treat the children in this school as if they were your own, and I think that's lovely.'

Sam's getting better. He's quieter; he's learning to read. Between the twin furies of his mother and his political masters, he will come through. Margaret gets angry more and more often, and how to deal with her rages is constantly in the back of Don's mind. I spent an afternoon at the hospital with her the other day — we thought she'd broken her arm — and one-to-one she was so charming, a beautiful girl, capable of childish games one minute, and almost adult conversation the next. We played games with advertisements in magazines, and she was as contemptuous as I was about the lengths people will go to so that you might buy something you don't want. They put her arm in a tight bandage, and I took her home, but no one was there.

Danielle writes better and better, and I'm going to send some of her work to *The Observer* Young Poets' competition, as soon as I've finished this. Simon peers at us through his pebbly glasses, like the professor he won't be. Anthony has left to go to Edinburgh Road, and I haven't seen him for ages. These are the owners of our schools, and if we let them down, we let everything down.